ACCIDENTAL POLITICIAN

By Adam Hattersley

GWN Publishing
GhostwritersNetwork.com

Accidental Politician

By Adam Hattersley

Published by: GWN Publishing | GWNPublishing.com

Edited by: Lil Barcaski and Linda Hinkle

Typesetting by: Cyndi Long | LongBar Creative Solutions

Cover Design by: Cyndi Long | GFADDesign.com

Cover Photo by: Nicholas Cardello

LongBar Creative Solutions | LongBarCreatives.com
GWN Publishing is a division of LongBar Creative Solutions, Inc.

ISBN-13: 978-1-7367932-3-7

AccidentalPolitician.com

For my wife, Christie. You have inspired me every day since we first met. None of this would have been possible without you.

Now, stop making me do stuff.

Contents

Foreword

by Bryan Farris

Rarely, in my 30 plus years of working in and around campaigns in the State of Florida, have I run across a candidate like Adam Hattersley. His integrity, compassion for others, and drive to "do the right thing," is seldom matched. These characteristics manifested themselves tenfold during his tenure in the Florida House of Representatives. Adam has become, not just my client, but a trusted and loyal friend ... a relationship that transcends and will long outlast our time on the Florida political scene. We weren't supposed to win that race in 2018 ... we were told time and time again that our chances were slim to none. We were denied funding at every level of the party apparatus, until the very end, when they thought we just might pull it off. This is best explained by the old adage, "Defeat is an orphan, but victory has 1,000 fathers." Determined to prove them all wrong, we doggedly forged ahead, not only winning, but making history as the least funded winning State House campaign in recent memory. We did it with pure grit, a stubborn refusal to accept defeat and, at least on my part, a little bit of spite. Our dedicated team of volunteers worked tirelessly, day in and day out, to elect a person we knew deserved a seat at the table. We knew that, by getting Adam elected, Florida would become a better place to live, work and play, just by him taking his values to Tallahassee. But none of the work, none of the drive, not even the most brilliant strategy, would have meant a thing without an amazing candidate. Adam filled that bill like no other and the rest, as they say, is history.

This book offers a candid, blunt, and humorous look at the campaign that we waged together. It pieces together Adam's thought process from before he and I ever met, artfully describes the rigors of the campaign, honestly discusses the many frustrations and roadblocks we faced along the way and, delightfully and emotionally, tells the tale of how it all came together and resulted in one of the best nights of my not-so-young life. If you've ever wondered how a campaign actually runs, with blunt honesty, this is the book you should read. If you would like to read the story of how a small campaign team became a family, this book is more than worth your time. I know you will enjoy reading it as much as I enjoyed living it.

Introduction

Before I discuss why I wrote this book, I want to describe a few details about my background to show you how unprepared I was for the world of politics.

I grew up in Littleton, CO (yes, that Littleton, CO of Columbine High School fame). I had a stay-at-home mom, a dad that worked far too much, and an older sister. I was one of those who thought school seemed easy. I never studied, rarely had homework, but sadly, didn't have the most active social life. In high school, I was in the choir – and we were good enough to perform in Carnegie Hall in New York on Easter Sunday in 1994.

Most of my time, however, was taken up by gymnastics. I started as a small child, and by my teens, was in the gym about 20 hours per week. I had dreams of the Olympics (unrealistic, I now realize) and competing in the NCAA. After graduating from high school, I fulfilled one of those dreams by competing for the University of Michigan and winning a National Championship with their team in 1999. I earned a B.S.E. in Aerospace Engineering in 2000, and an M.S.E. in Aerospace Engineering in 2001. Yes, I am a rocket scientist.

Following in my father's footsteps, I joined the military after college. However, instead of the Army like my dad, I joined the "better" service, the U.S. Navy. I was commissioned as a Naval Officer three weeks before the September 11th attacks in 2001, and after nuclear propulsion training, served as a Submarine Officer. After three years on the USS COLUMBUS (SSN 762), I became an instructor at the U.S. Naval Academy in their Electrical Engineering Department. I'm a nerd through and through.

During my time at the Academy, I volunteered to go to Iraq with an Army unit. I went on over 200 combat missions, and was there at the height of the war, with the second half of my year-long tour covering the famous "surge." Service is in my family's blood, but after eight years, I felt I had done my part and left the Navy in 2008.

That autumn, my wife, Christie, and I moved to Sydney, Australia (she had gotten a job there) for a year, before coming back to the U.S. and settling in Tampa, Florida for a job I had gotten. I worked for a Fortune 500 company for seven years managing employees all over the world. Although I had never been that interested in politics, but because public service was still important to me, I was in search of the best way to incorporate that yearning into my work life.

Although my wife and I started our own small business in 2016, it wasn't as fulfilling as my time in the Navy. In 2017, I was appointed to the Selective Service Board by the Governor of Florida, but it didn't really meet my desire to serve. (It's mostly a "token" appointment because when was the last time we had a military draft?)

Why do I tell you all of this? Not to just give you some understanding of who I am, but to give you a sense of what motivated my decision to dive in and get involved in politics.

Service.

It had been ingrained in me since I was a child. Like many people, I wanted to earn my right to enjoy the benefits of being an American. Had I done that with eight years in the military and multiple deployments? Maybe. But was that enough to make me feel like I really deserved what we have in this country? I wasn't so sure.

Some people have called me naïve, or sometimes a blind idealist (if they want to be kind). But when it comes right down to it, this country needs people to serve, and however rare that mindset is, and the closer those people are to idealists, the better they can be of service. I only wish there were more of us. I wrote this book in hopes of finding other service-minded optimists like myself and help them avoid some of my land mines and/or follow some of the paths I managed to forge.

If you are naïve like me, or prefer to be a blind idealist, then I have news for you. You may be just the type of person we need in government. Government work doesn't always involve the flashy stuff you see on TV, but the real nitty gritty stuff that impacts peoples' lives. Local and state offices have more effect on you than any other type of political office but are typically swept under the rug in the modern news cycle as if they don't matter. They do. Immensely. It may not be "sexy," but oftentimes it matters far more than what happens in Washington, D.C. Believe it or not, D.C. is not the center of the political world even though it is easy to think that.

Getting the chance to serve in such a capacity is a challenge; you have to win the office first. There are a lot of moving parts to a campaign, and a lot of unexpected things to overcome. How to start? How to file the right paperwork? How to raise the resources you'll need to have a shot? Even what goes into making the decision to run is more complicated than what you see in the movies or hear about on TV. This is serious business, and there's an entire industry built around it. Heck, there's a whole culture built around it. Who are the right people to even ask where to begin?

One thing a non-political person is always surprised about is how much capital it takes to run even a small campaign. For better or worse, money is, unfortunately, still a major driver in elections. Travel, communication, advertising, mail, staff and more all take money. And time, lots of it. Not to spoil the ending, but I was victorious in a State House race with the lowest fundraising total of any winner for a contested seat in my first campaign. How did we do it?

Well, if you'd like to find out, you need to turn the page.

CHAPTER ONE

"Fix It!"

Adam on the bridge of the USS COLUMBUS (SSN 762)
Photo used with courtesy of the Hattersley Family

Chapter 1:

"Fix it!"

So, there I was... this is a no shitter.

That's how all good Navy stories, or how all old Navy sailors telling a story, start. This "no shitter" story started in Estero, FL on March 10, 2018. I was doing what I did most weekends between the months of December and April, judging gymnastics competitions. This particular weekend it was the Florida Boy's Gymnastics State Championships (I'll get to that in a minute). I was watching the competition with my judge's eagle eye when my wife called. I was surprised to see her number appear on my cell phone during a competition.

"I'm not sure what's going on, but I've gotten a bunch of phone calls today from people I don't know asking if you will run for a seat in the state legislature," she said, with not a small amount of confusion in her voice.

"What? From who? For what?" was about all I could muster in response.

But I'll get back to this later, too.

***

I am a politician. I didn't set out to be one, it just kind of happened. It was almost an accident. Throughout my life I had flirted with the idea of going into politics, but ultimately thought it would be far too much trouble for what it was worth. Why bother with the headache? It's not like government had ever actually worked for me or anyone I knew. What was the point?

Neither my wife, Christie, nor I had ever been particularly political. We made sure to vote in every November election, but since we weren't registered with a political party, we couldn't vote in Florida's primary elections (Florida is a closed primary state, meaning only people registered with a party can vote in that party's primary). That world seemed so far away and nothing we saw on TV coming out of Washington, D.C. seemed to matter.

We watched the 2016 presidential campaigns like most Americans. Interested, but fairly certain of the outcome. Who in their right mind would vote for a crazy reality TV show personality? And even though the polls were looking good for the United States to get its first female president, my wife wanted to make sure that it actually happened. She said she needed to do everything she could to make sure Hillary was elected and Trump was not, so she volunteered to go door-to-door for the Hilary campaign. She felt good about finally getting a little involved in the process – like she was making a difference and was a part of this exciting story.

Election night 2016 arrived and we invited about 30 people to our house for a watch party. The mood went from light and optimistic in the early hours, to dark and depressed by the time we kicked everyone out around 10 p.m. What had just happened? How had Trump won? Christie spent the next three days crying, and on the fourth day she simply looked at me and said "Fix it." I hated not being able to help her, but what did she expect me to do?

Things calmed down over the next few weeks, and I began traveling all over the county judging gymnastics competitions, like I did every winter (I said I would get back to this). I had been a gymnast for nearly 20 years, competing for the University of Michigan, and was also a member of the 1999 NCAA National Championship Team. I had been a judge since 1996 and was steadily rising in the judicial ranks. The previous summer, I even had the opportunity to judge the simulated Olympics with the U.S. team before they went to Rio.

So, after the election disappointment, our lives spun steadily back into relative normality. But Christie's request to "fix it" never really left my subconscious.

In mid-February I was in Atlanta, driving a rental car from the airport to a gymnastics competition. The local radio station played a commercial for a congressional race. It was only February! Jesus, it's only been a few months since the last election, I thought. I couldn't believe how early these big campaigns started. I hadn't realized that there was a special election being held in Georgia in April, but that just goes to illustrate my ignorance of all things political. That commercial got me wondering though.

How would a person put a political campaign together? Could being an elected official help me to "fix it"? I resolved to speak with Christie when I got home a couple of days later.

That conversation ended up being pretty stagnant. When it came down to it, neither of us had the slightest clue as to who to talk to, how to start, or even where to look for that kind of information. I chalked it up to a whim, so without having wasted much time, we decided to drop it. After all, our lives were pretty good, there was no real or pressing need to rock the boat.

Every. Single. One.

Fast forward to August of 2017. I had been selected as the US judge for the World University Games in Taipei, Taiwan. This event is huge – the second largest multi-sport event in the world, next to only the Olympic Games. I was super excited. It was only my second formal international judging assignment representing the United States, and it was a big one (*a 9.7 from the American judge!*). I landed in Taipei with the U.S. team, but as an official, I was whisked away to stay in the hotel with all the other officials, while the team went off to the Athletes' Village. *Very cool.*

It was a relatively short ride to the hotel, and after getting my room, I went through the Games' check-in process. At every check-in station I visited, every single one, I heard a joke about Donald Trump. Every. Single. One.

At our first judges' meeting, saying hello to all the other officials from all over the world, every single one mentioned our recent election with a shock or a laugh. Every. Single. One.

Do keep in mind, I served nearly eight years in the United States Navy, deployed several times, and even did a tour on the ground in Iraq with an Army unit. I am proud of my country and proud of my service. Those jabs hurt.

What happened to the America that was the envy of the world? Were we really that much of a laughingstock in the international community? When our president is the butt of jokes from even the Norwegian judge (a very cool guy, and thrice voted Norway's Fittest Man), something is definitely wrong.

When I returned home, I reopened the conversation of public service that we thought was dead. I was embarrassed by the state of our country, and felt like I owed it to myself to at least look into what we could do. Luckily, Christie had a friend who had long ties to local politics in Polk County just north of us. Polk County made up about one-third of the congressional district that I lived in, so it was a great place to start. I didn't even know what races were available, but since everyone saw things coming out of Washington, D.C. on TV and in the newspaper, I figured looking into running for congress was a natural place to start.

Christie's friend, Jane, did indeed have long ties to Polk County. Her family had been deeply involved in the community for years, and she had relationships with dozens of important local leaders. She set up three days of meetings, about 20 in all, for me to get to know who was who in the district and get an idea of what a congressional campaign would entail.

Most of the people we met with were exceedingly kind, but everyone had a different issue or agenda, and they were convinced that THEIR issue was absolutely the most important one in Central Florida. And the thing is, they were right. Nearly all of their issues were big and important. From crumbling infrastructure to the hotbed of human trafficking, the troubles in our district ran the full gamut.

We were not so subtly warned that we would need to "cleanse" our social media (remove any embarrassing photos or posts, and even any photos with something as simple as alcohol in them), dig into our pasts for anything, no matter how small, that could be used as an attack against us. It was overwhelming! Going from "zero to 60 in under two seconds" kind of overwhelming. Not to mention the cost of running a congressional campaign. We found out that we would need to raise a minimum of four million dollars to have a real shot at making up the eleven-point Republican margin of victory (based on the 2016 election). If we weren't intimidated before, we certainly were now. Running for political office sounded absolutely, positively, insane. No one in their right mind would want to do it.

We. Were. Out.

Off the Hook

Some of the people we met with, though, asked if we had spoken to another young Navy veteran named Andrew Learned. Apparently, he was just about to file to run for the same seat that I was considering, Florida's Congressional District 15. That was great! Someone with a similar background to mine who was already running. I felt like I'd been let off the hook to "fix it" because a mini-me was already on the hunt. We got his contact info and set up a coffee date.

We met a couple weeks later and talked for about an hour. He seemed like a put together guy who, besides being a Navy veteran, also owned his own business (again, just like me). He was a little more progressive than I was, but we aligned on most issues. There on the spot, Christie and I decided that that was how we would get involved, by helping a candidate run for the congressional seat and supporting candidates we believed in. We told Andrew we would host a "house party" (small fundraiser) for him at our home.

We had never hosted a candidate fundraiser before and didn't really know where to start. Luckily, a house party style fundraiser is extremely easy to put together. It is, at its core, a get together with friends. We invited about 45 people (knowing only about 30 would show up), which is a good to large sized house party for political novices. Food, drinks, snacks, and ... politics! Who could resist, right? Even better, Christie and I had a bit of a reputation for throwing a good party based on the annual wine-tasting events we had put on for almost a decade. If we couldn't get 30 people for a Hattersley Party, then we weren't trying hard enough (even if the attendees knew the reason for the gathering was political in nature).

Six weeks after first meeting Andrew, we held the fundraiser. Like I said, it was mostly a bunch of our friends (new people Andrew hadn't met, so that was a plus) hanging out, eating, drinking, and having a good time. The only difference was that about an hour into the festivities, I ushered everyone into our kitchen to listen to Andrew talk for about five minutes on why he was running for Congress, and what he wanted/hoped to accomplish when he won (a "stump" speech). About 10 minutes of question and answers followed, then I spent a minute asking if people would donate to his campaign, after which, back to normal party mode.

Fundraising wise, it wasn't a very successful event for Andrew. But he did ask me if I knew anyone who would be willing to flesh out the "down-ballot" (local races were considered "down the ballot" from the higher ones) races for the Democratic ticket. For the 2018 election, there still weren't any Democrats registered for several races that would cover our neighborhood. He even asked my neighbor if he would run for the Soil and Water Conservation Board. The answer he got was, of course, "What the hell is that?"

After most of the attendees left, Andrew asked me if I knew anyone who would consider running for any position at all. I told him that if the timeline was getting too short, to give me a call to talk about what roles were still needed. I'd served before, and it was a door I figured I would leave open. In most cases, when you tell someone "call me if you need me," it's just a courtesy offer. Like, "Yeah, if you need anything, just let me know." Oftentimes, in fact, most times, people don't actually call in those favors.

So, there I was, four months later... in Estero, FL on March 10, 2018, judging the Florida Boy's Gymnastics State Championships. Any thoughts of politics were long gone from my head when my wife called.

"I'm not sure what's going on, but I've gotten a bunch of phone calls today from people I don't know asking if you will run for a seat in the state legislature," she said, not a small amount of confusion in her voice.

"What? From who? For what?" was about all I could muster in response. My offer of a favor was about to be called in.

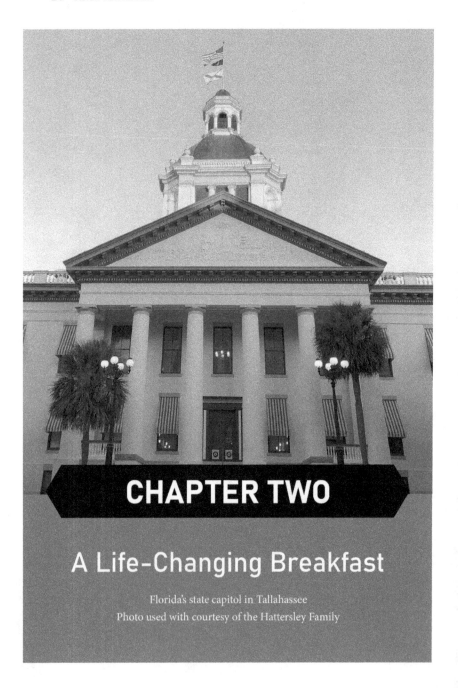

CHAPTER TWO

A Life-Changing Breakfast

Florida's state capitol in Tallahassee
Photo used with courtesy of the Hattersley Family

Chapter 2:

A Life-Changing Breakfast

My brief phone conversation with my wife was weighing on my mind. Her words echoed in my head as the competition finished but I was perplexed and needed more information. Someone had the idea that I should run for something? Why me? What made me a better potential candidate than anyone else? Christie's unsolicited calls from the weekend would certainly be our biggest topic of discussion when I got home. Well, after telling her all the juicy gym gossip from my weekend away, (okay, there wasn't really any juicy gossip). I had barely set my bags down when Christie launched into the rundown of her weekend conversations.

Comments from Christie:

Per usual that time of year, Adam was off judging gymnastics, so I was home by myself from Thursday night until Sunday evening. I took advantage of the alone time the way I normally did by scheduling dinner with girlfriends, enjoying an outdoor workout, and cuddling on the couch with our dog, Patton, to watch a RomCom. Like most men, Adam is not the RomCom type.

I was about halfway through a movie when my phone rang. It was the dreaded "unknown caller" and I almost didn't answer. But being a salesperson, I usually try to give other salespeople time, hoping for the same courtesy in return. To my surprise, it wasn't a salesperson. It was a lawyer named Erica Anderson. I did not know her or why she was calling randomly on a Saturday morning.

"Hi, is Adam Hatters ... Hat ... Hat-ter-sloy there?" she asked me.

"No, this is his wife, Christie HATTERSLEY" I tried to correct her pronunciation in my introduction. Our last name is a little tough, and that happens all the time. "Adam isn't here at the moment. May I ask who's calling?"

"Oh, well, can I talk to you? I got your name from some people on Facebook who said he might run for the Florida House. Tell me he's going to run."

"Excuse me? Got his name from who?" I asked, unable to hide the surprise in my voice.

"That doesn't really matter, what does matter is that we NEED someone to run in House District 59. Do you know who Ronda Storms is? Do you know what she did the last time she was in office? She just filed to run for Florida House District 59. She's known for her history of anti-LGBTQ activism. She's the reason Tampa cancelled Pride for so many years. She's an extreme, far-right evangelical and besides wanting to ban the LGBTQ community, she wants to ban all women's choice! We have to find someone to run against her and someone suggested you or Adam might run," Erica said.

"First off, who is this 'we' you keep referencing?"

"The Democratic Party. We need a Democrat in the race."

"I'm flattered you called, and I'll talk to Adam about it because I have a full-time job, and he's probably the best choice given he's a Navy veteran, but honestly, even if he did run, we wouldn't even know where to start."

"That doesn't matter either. Call Bryan Farris, and he'll explain everything. I'll text you his number."

Erica seemed exasperated, almost confused as to why I was pushing back on this conversation. I asked who Bryan was and she said that he was really into politics and could walk us through the process. I promised that we would call this Bryan person and at least hear him out. She finished the conversation with *"Please run. Please tell me he'll run."* I replied by saying that I would have a serious conversation with my husband and would keep her posted.

I was totally confused by the whole conversation and still had very little understanding of who this "Bryan person" was or how he would be able to explain everything. I assumed he was some sort of local political guru or shaman because that's what Erica made him sound like.

Over the next day and a half, I got three more random messages from people on various platforms – some I knew and some I didn't – about Adam running for office and stopping this Ronda person from destroying individual rights in Florida.

✳✳✳

As Christie described the remainder of her weekend conversations, I was more and more surprised. When she first told me about it, it seemed like a joke, but it turned out to be a much greater recruiting effort than I realized. I asked her who Bryan was and what he did.

"I dunno," she said. "Erica just said to call him, and he'd tell you what to do."

While still in my thoughts, I put it off for a day or two to deal with other issues that needed tending to in my business. Eventually, I worked up the courage to call this Bryan person who would walk me through the political world or at least give me some more context.

Since Christie had promised Erica Anderson that I would follow up, I felt obligated. I dialed the number that Erica had forced on Christie and an unfamiliar voice answered.

"Hah-llllllooo?" (this will become a familiar phone greeting).

"Hi, is Bryan available?"

"This is Bryan."

"My name is Adam Hattersley. I got your number from someone named Erica Anderson. She wanted me to call you to talk about running for the Florida House?" At this point, I was so wary and confused that almost every one of my statements was in question form.

"Oh yeah, she told me you'd be calling. Look, I really doubt you're the right guy or would even be a good candidate, but Erica thinks we should meet and talk about it." This conversation was already just oozing confidence in my potential candidacy – great. "I'm pretty busy, but maybe we can meet for lunch. Can you come to South Tampa tomorrow around noon? I'm not going all the way out to East county."

"Fine, I guess," was my lukewarm reply.

Old Florida Setting with a New Florida Reality

Christie and I decided we may as well hear what this guy had to say, even if it seemed like he did not want to say it to us. We agreed to lunch the following day, and yes, we would drive to Bryan for his convenience. He picked a place, and we were officially scheduled.

Christie and I had watched a lot of the *West Wing* and saw that everyone in the political world seemed to wear a suit. We were in Florida, so we both opted for business casual but wanted to make a good impression. Christie suggested I dress for the job I wanted, not the job I had, so I wore a Polo shirt and nice slacks, and she wore a dress. Even if this led to nothing, we wanted to be as professional about it as possible.

The next day, we rolled up to where we were meeting Bryan for lunch—a small, straight-out-of-the-'60s, pastel-colored, South Tampa motel called the Tahitian Inn. Picture the motel the astronauts stayed at in the Disney series, "The Right Stuff." It couldn't have been more Florida cliché if it tried. And yes, it came complete with real (and fake) palm trees both inside and out. There was a small diner on the first floor, and its greasy spoon atmosphere was exactly on-brand for the establishment. The faux AstroTurf in the hallway greatly added to the motif.

Keep in mind, we had never met Bryan, or seen a photo of him. We had absolutely NO idea who we were looking for. Christie and I are (usually) always on time. Unbeknownst to us, Bryan is (usually) always late so, we were left wandering around looking like confused tourists for about 15 minutes until a slightly pudgy, middle-aged guy in khaki shorts and flip flops walked in.

"Bryan?" I asked, secretly hoping this was not the guy.

"Yes, Hi," he responded, sticking a hand out to shake mine.

"I'm Adam, and this is my wife, Christie," I replied as we shook hands, "Thanks for meeting with us."

"No problem, wanna grab a table? I'm going to go have a cigarette, be back in a minute."

Not a very auspicious start, but we decided to roll with it. Bryan headed out to the back patio, pack of cigarettes in hand, while Christie and I snagged a table. Even though the place wasn't that big, it seemed to be pretty popular with the locals, so the only available table was smack dab in the middle of the dining room. Not ideal for a private conversation, but it would have to do. Christie and I each grabbed one of the single-page, laminated menus deciding if breakfast or lunch was more appropriate (she chose lunch, I went with breakfast as it's hard for me to resist a good waffle).

Bryan returned right as the waitress was taking our drink orders. He gave her what must have been his usual order since he didn't look at the menu. With no hesitation and plenty of enthusiasm, he dove straight into his soliloquy on the topic of the FL 59 race and a little bit of history.

"Okay, here's the deal. The current Representative is running for Congress, so it's now an open seat. There are two Republicans running against each other in the 59th in the primary, and so far, no Democrat. The two R's (Bryan tended to refer to Republicans simply as "R's", and Democrats as "D's") are Joe Wicker, who's been running since last September, and Ronda Storms, who filed last week. I think that Joe is a typical gun-crazy, anti-fun Republican, but Ronda is a whole different story," Bryan spit out with no preamble. "Just so you know, I'm gay, and Ronda is ... how should I put it delicately ... the enemy of the gay community."

I told him that Erica had briefed Christie on that particular situation, but Bryan kept going.

"I have friends out that way that were getting death threats from her supporters, and they ended up having to move away for their own safety. Trust me, Erica only told you a portion of the story. The LGBTQ community is outraged! Heck, I'm betting you know that most of the convention hospitality industry across the country is gay, and Storms' "anti-Pride" and "gay banning" efforts led to an unofficial national boycott of the city for events from which we still haven't recovered. It's not just a social issue; it's an economic one!"

"I get it," I said. "Christie's brother is gay, and we helped him, and his husband when they adopted a baby here in Florida last year. No one is going to make our family illegal."

That piqued Bryan's attention, but he was still extremely skeptical. "Look, the last election in 2016 didn't go very well for us out there. The Republican won that district by nearly nine points. I don't know if you'd be the right person for this. What makes you think you could do any better?" he asked. "What's your background?"

"Well, first off, I don't know if I can do better, and I'm not sure if I want to run," I said, figuring honesty was always the best policy.

"Let's say you wanted to run," he started. "Give me a one-minute elevator speech that would sell me on voting for you."

"Okay, so, I grew up in Littleton, CO, yup, home of Columbine High School infamy, and no, I didn't go there. I went to the University of Michigan and was on their men's gymnastics team. We were the 1999 NCAA team national champions. I have bachelor's and master's degrees in Aerospace Engineering – basically rocket science – and after college, I went into the U.S. Navy. I was commissioned as an officer about three weeks before September 11, 2001. I went through the nuclear power and submarine training pipelines and spent three years on a Los Angeles Class Attack Submarine. I did a six-month Western Pacific deployment on that boat out of Pearl Harbor, Hawaii, and then we did a change of homeport to the shipyard in Bremerton, Washington. After my time on the submarine, I became an electrical engineering instructor at the U.S. Naval Academy in Annapolis, Maryland, and subsequently volunteered for a year-long combat tour in Iraq with an Army unit. I was there from 2006 to 2007, and the second half of my tour was during the famous "surge" – it got pretty chippy around then. After I got home and finished my time teaching at the Academy, Christie and I got married and moved to Australia for a year where she'd been offered a job. We moved here to Tampa in 2009, when I got a job with a GE subsidiary. When GE bought a big European company, my whole department was laid off because we were considered redundant. After that, I started a small business and have been doing that for the past few years."

I paused. Bryan paused. Christie hates pauses, so she chimed in.

"He was awarded a Bronze Star for his time in Iraq," she said, smiling broadly. She's very proud of this fact about me.

Bryan slammed his hand on the table and stopped the conversation short. "Whoa, whoa ... you have a Bronze Star?" He laughed out loud maniacally. "You're a political consultant's wet dream!"

Well, this chat had quickly changed its course, albeit a tad inappropriately. Bryan was all in now, even if Christie and I weren't quite there yet.

"Okay! We need to open a campaign bank account and you need to start raising money right away," he continued. "I'll help you file to run as soon as possible. Also, start attending the county party meetings, the different Democratic clubs, the caucus meetings, and definitely the DEC meeting."

"Hold on!" I jumped in. "I have no idea how to raise money for a political campaign! Besides, I'm still not sure I even want to run. You said we would be starting nine points down? How could I possibly win if I did run? Heck, I'm not even a Democrat! And I certainly don't know what a DEC meeting is." As you can see, I was trying to slow things down a bit.

"First off, the DEC is the Democratic Executive Committee – basically the county party, but don't worry about any of that," Bryan said. "I'll make some calls to figure out the 'not a Democrat' thing – how are you not a Democrat? But you really need to decide whether or not you want to run. I think you should, and I can help you. I'm going to need a decision in the next couple days so we can get things rolling. I'm also going to talk to the DEC and stop candidate recruiting for this race. I'm not sure if they're really even trying since they've given up on that part of the county. When you decide to run, I want to avoid a primary and give you a clear field." He was definitely on a roll now. "I'm also going to introduce you to my campaign partner, Chris Mitchell. He runs a digital political advertising company and does a great job. He can do your digital, and I'll be your general consultant. Once you raise some money, we can look at hiring some campaign staff."

"Wait ... What is a general consultant? What does that even mean?" Christie asked.

"A general consultant, or GC, is one of, if not the, go-to person for a campaign. They help develop strategy, help navigate the current players in the party, help with filings and forms. They take care of just about anything the campaign needs. I'm already working on a couple other campaigns and want to pick up a couple more for this cycle. Think of the GC as you would a general manager of a professional football team," Bryan explained.

"I thought that was a campaign manager?" I tentatively asked.

"Not really. Keeping on with the professional sports reference, the campaign manager is more like the head coach. They work with the candidate and do the day-to-day tasks. The GC absolutely works with the campaign manager, but in more of a strategic role. We'll have to find you a campaign manager soon, though. First, you have to raise money."

"You keep saying I have to raise money! How is that important? How would I even go about starting that?" I really was naïve at this point.

"WHAT?" Bryan exclaimed, almost choking on his lunch. "What do you mean, how is that important! Without money, we can't hire a staff, we can't buy online ads, or any ads, for that matter. No swag with your name or logo – and by the way, you're going to need a logo. Nothing! No one will have a clue who you are unless we communicate with them. And we can't communicate if we don't have any money. Mail, digital ads, texting, phone calls, people out on the street knocking on doors for you, radio, and if we're lucky, TV. It all takes money."

"You mean, you can't get paid if he doesn't raise any money," Christie added. My wife has a way of getting right to the point, doesn't she?

"Well, yes. That too," Bryan admitted.

"Exactly how much money are we talking about, here?"

"For a state representative race like this? To be competitive, in a Republican district ... just spit-balling, but I would guess about $300,000. Chris and I can write a campaign plan and do a deeper dive on it and come up with a more accurate number. In 2016, the Democratic candidate raised about $200,000 and the Republican raised just shy of $375,000 – so yeah, to be competitive $300,000 is a good ballpark figure. We have to flip a lot of votes," said Bryan, far too casually.

Tick Count Starts

$300,000! Was he insane?! For a job (I would later find out) that only pays $29,000 per year, a person must raise more than 10 times that amount just to get it! What the hell is wrong with American politics if you need that kind of money to earn the "privilege" to serve?

"I don't even know how to get started raising $100, let alone $300,000," I said, feeling a bit overwhelmed. That daunting amount was definitely a tick in the 'con' column when Christie and I discussed this decision. "How would I even start doing something like that?" Due to my inexperience with the political process, I was just so shocked by that seemingly impossible number.

"Easy. Go through every single person you've ever known, call them, and ask them for money. That's how you start. You have some rich friends, right? In Florida, the most a person can give you is $1,000 before the primary election date, and $1,000 after," he said, once again, far too nonchalantly in my opinion.

First off, I didn't have any rich friends. Secondly, even if I did, I had no idea how to go about asking someone for $1,000!

"Oh, and you may want to start by loaning the campaign some money yourself to show that you're serious. $3,000 would be a good start. And, if you have money in the campaign account left over after the election, you can pay yourself back," said Bryan, doing his part to reassure me.

Wait a minute, not only am I going to swallow some of my pride by asking my friends for money, which felt like begging to me, but I would have to kick in several thousand dollars myself right at the start, and who knows how much more throughout the process? This was sounding worse and worse. No wonder it seems like only wealthy people ever run for office! They're the only ones who can afford to! Not to mention the time that would have to go into raising money and attending events, which would be more than a full-time job in and of itself. Running a campaign like this, with the intent to win or why else run, would nearly preempt anyone's ability to hold a regular job. Bryan wasn't just asking me to run, he was asking me to completely alter my life (and my bank account and quite possibly, my friendships). What the hell had we gotten ourselves into? Another tick in the 'con' column.

"Look, this is not a small undertaking. I get that. But I think you have a shot. We need someone willing to stand up to this Republican bully and defend people who can't defend themselves," explained Bryan who was now getting serious.

"Christie and I need to discuss this, okay? It's a big decision, a life-changing decision. We're going to need some time." I was pumping the brakes as hard as I could at this point.

"Don't take too much time figuring this out. It's already late in the game to file, and every day you delay is another day you're not raising money. I'm not going to lie; the party was not even looking to challenge this race based on the last election's results, but now with this anti-LGBTQ person running, we have to put up a fight – even if it's one we'll probably lose." Again, cue Bryan with the confidence (or lack thereof) and add another tick to the 'con' column.

"Thanks for meeting with us. I'll be sure to give you a call in the next few days with a decision," I told him as we paid our check and headed out.

What the hell were we thinking about getting ourselves into? 'We have to put up a fight – even if it's one we'll probably lose'? This seemed like a pretty daunting line of work to get into, a lot of effort with big potential for heart-crushing defeat and NOT something I (or any sane person) would typically pursue.

Christie and I got in the car to head home. She looked at me and said, "We can't let the Republicans win. You need to fix it."

Goddamnit. At the very least, that first meeting taught me that I had absolutely no idea how our politicians get to where they are or how our political system actually works.

Adam's fundraising total: $0

Joe's fundraising total: $28,562

Ronda's fundraising total: $0

"SEND ME."

CHAPTER THREE

Decisions and Diving In

A little joke after volunteering to go to Iraq
Photo used with courtesy of the Hattersley Family

Chapter 3:

Decisions and Diving In

The big "decision discussion" started in the car on the way home from that first meeting with Bryan. First, being us, we chatted about the pros and cons of the restaurant – the food, the atmosphere, the food. We keep a running tally of eateries in the greater Tampa area, and let's be honest, that came first.

Next came the pros and cons of running for office. The con column already had several entries: fundraising, potentially kicking in our own money, fundraising, embarrassment of asking friends and family for money, fundraising, starting nine points down with no plan to pick up ground, fundraising, my new full-time job is campaigning, fundraising ... and ... did I mention fundraising?

Christie and I could easily come up with even more things to add to the con list. Putting one's life on public display is never an appetizing concept, for one thing. Opening yourself, and your family, up to potentially vicious public attacks and lies is not on many people's bucket lists. Not to mention we had no idea who the players in the Tampa area were. We would be forced at least initially, to solely rely on Bryan's opinion of his own knowledge, which as a former naval officer and engineer, would be extremely difficult for me to do. Another big reason was the possible (and as the data showed, probable) risk of losing epically on election night. Oh, and have I put fundraising in the con column, already?

The pro column, by contrast, was short: there wasn't one.

Christie and I sat in silence for a while.

"Have I ever told you about my experience on September 11th?" I asked her.

"No. You don't talk about your time in the military very much," she said. I guess that's one way in which I resemble my father, who in over 50 years, has never spoken (to me) about his time in Vietnam.

"Well, this isn't so much a war story," I said.

***

Military Flashback

September 11, 2001. I had been commissioned as an officer in the U.S. Navy about three weeks prior, and was back in Ann Arbor, MI doing what was called OHARP (the Officer Home Area Recruiting Program, the military loves a good acronym) while I was waiting for my first post-commissioning school to start. I was slated to be a nuclear submarine officer, and that has a hefty training program, starting with six months in Charleston, S.C. at the Naval Nuclear Power School, then six months at the Naval Nuclear Power Training Command (NNPTC), which we called "Prototype." It's a real, living and breathing naval nuclear reactor on land where new personnel learn to operate and stand watch. After that, I was scheduled to do three months in Groton, C.T. at the Submarine Officers'

Basic Course. That all needed to be successfully completed before joining the fleet.

My Nuke School class (besides acronyms, the military also likes a good nickname) didn't start until November and the Navy is loathe to let anyone sit idle for three months. So, I was sent back to where I joined up to help convince other people to join up. Makes sense, especially since I was now the resident expert on how to complete Officer Candidate School and earn a commission, having just finished it. I was in a unique position to let new officer recruits know exactly what to expect and hopefully give them a leg up to success.

While I was driving to the office, the radio DJ was talking about a plane crashing into the World Trade Center in New York, but they didn't have many details. I just figured it was a small, one-person propeller-driven plane that had a bad pilot. What else could it be? When I walked into the office though, my interim boss had the TV on so he brought me up to speed on what had happened thus far. He was just finishing explaining what he had heard when a second plane flew into the as-yet-untouched tower live on the screen in front of us. Five minutes later, the recruiting station got a call from our district headquarters sending everyone home for the day and telling us to stay on alert.

Before he sent everyone home, my boss looked at me and said, "Have you ever seen the photos from the day after the Pearl Harbor attack in 1941? Recruiting stations had lines out the door and around the block. Come in early tomorrow and be ready for a flood of people who want to join up and defend the country." He was right; this was my generation's Pearl Harbor moment.

The next morning, the entire staff was in early, uniforms freshly pressed. We got extra brochures out of storage, added extra chairs to the waiting area, and even printed more copies of the job description one-pagers that were almost never looked at. We had all our bases covered and were ready for our own surge. When 9 a.m. rolled around, we opened the office, but no one was waiting outside.

Understandable. We were near a college town and things usually took a little longer to get going. We figured most people of military age had early classes at either my Alma Mater, the University of Michigan, or at nearby Eastern Michigan University. We probably wouldn't see any of them before lunch. We ordered lunch so we could eat in, more of a working lunch, but the midday meal came and went without a single person coming to the office. After several more time-related excuses, the clock chimed 6 p.m. Grand total of appearances at the U.S. Navy's only officer recruiting station within 50 miles the day after the largest attack against the United States in decades: zero.

We were shocked. What happened? Where was everyone? Why was this not our version of December 8th, 1941? We were determined to find out, so the next day my boss and I went to the center of campus at the University of Michigan to ask people what they thought about what was happening in the world and to our country.

The prevailing answer we received: "Yeah, it's terrible, but 'they' will do something about it".

"They." Hmm... I wonder who they thought who they were.

✳✳✳

"That day has always stuck with me," I said. "Remember, in 2006, before we were together, when I told you that I had volunteered to go to Iraq? I was thinking about

September 12th, 2001. I was thinking that the "they" people always seem to rely on comes from ... us. And if I wasn't going to stand up when it was needed, who would? I couldn't count on a mythical 'they.' I had to do it."

"Well," Christie added, "if you're not part of the solution, you're part of the problem. And we CAN'T let a person who would make our niece illegal just walk into a position of power. You're right, 'they' comes from 'us'."

That one idea seemed to have outweighed the entire con column we had just spent an hour and a half making.

The next morning, I called Bryan to tell him that I was in.

"Hah-llllllooo?" Bryan's distinctive telephone greeting rang through as he picked up the phone.

"Hi, it's Adam Hattersley – I'll do it, I'll run in the 59th. Now what?"

"That's great! There may be a problem though. Yesterday afternoon I checked online and apparently if a person is going to run under a party affiliation, they have to have been a member of that party for a minimum of one year before Election Day. I'm freaking out because you're the perfect candidate for this seat! Before we go any further, let me make some calls and check to see if you can even file to run," he told me.

Well, that was pretty damn anticlimactic! Christie and I had gone through quite a decision-making process over the past week since she'd gotten those first recruiting phone calls, and now maybe it was all for naught. Bryan told me he would call me back in the next few hours with what the rules actually said, but for now, everything was already on pause. I filled Christie in on what Bryan said, almost laughing at how my potential political career may have already been over. All these little details really do show how complicated running for office can be. At that point, I didn't even know what I didn't know.

There wasn't much else to do but go about our day, maybe a little more relaxed, but at the same time, maybe a little more tense. This wouldn't be the first time diametrically opposing emotions would be sharing space in my head over the next several months. I had a promotional products business to run, and I was flying to Boston in a few weeks to judge a large, multi-state gymnastics competition and then going to Ann Arbor to judge an NCAA competition, so I had plenty to do to keep my mind off my now uncertain future.

Luckily, Bryan called back a few hours later. "We're good!" he shouted. "I called the Secretary of State's office and spoke to an election lawyer. Since you were not registered with a party at all, that's called 'NPA' or 'No Party Affiliation'. You're good to go! The year-long party membership rule is only for people switching parties. So, what I need you to do RIGHT NOW is go on the county Supervisor of Elections website and update your voter registration as Democrat. Christie probably should, too."

"I was almost relieved that I might not be able to run, but okay. After updating my registration, what do we do next?" I asked.

"I'll go onto the Secretary of State's website and download the forms we need to officially file. It's actually pretty simple - only three forms. The 'Statement of Candidate,' which is an acknowledgement that you have access to read the campaign finance laws; the 'Candidate Oath,' that tells the State you intend to run and in what district; and the 'Appointment of Campaign Treasurer' form, that lets the State know who is handling your campaign account, and what bank holds it. By the way, for all my campaigns, I use the same CPA as Campaign Treasurer to make it easy – and he's really good. So that's already covered."

Bryan described what seemed like a fairly easy process, but, if you didn't have a 'Bryan' type helping, how would a person know what they needed or where to look?

"Oh, and we won't officially file until the first Monday in April. Since March is half over, we want our first fundraising opportunity to be a full month. That way you get as much time as possible to raise as much money as possible for our first finance report. That gives us time to get the accounts all set up, which, by the way, you need to identify what bank you want to use TOMORROW, but don't actually open the account until we sign the filing papers," Bryan emphasized. "However, don't wait for the account to be set up or the paperwork to go through. Start calling your friends to let them know you're running and to ask them to pledge some money to support the campaign. That way, when we're ready to 'go live' in April, you'll have a line of people ready to donate. Think of it as a jumpstart on fundraising. In the meantime, I'm going to email you a list of local Democratic Club and Caucus meetings you should start attending. The first one should be the County DEC meeting next week. I can start introducing you around to the people you're going to need to know. And when I see you there, can you... um... sign a contract with me as your General Consultant?"

That was a huge download of information. My head was swimming with all the 'head on fire' immediate tasks that needed doing and how I had very little idea of how to do any of it. I told Bryan to email over a draft contract, and asked if there were any other things he could think of for me to get ready to run for office. For simplicity's sake, let's do this in list form:

1. Officially change party registration to Democrat

2. Find a bank for the campaign account

3. Go through everyone I've ever met and let them know I'm running for office, ask for their (eventual) financial support

4. Start logo design

5. Schedule every political club and caucus meeting I can find to attend

6. Figure out a campaign slogan or catch phrase

7. Determine three or four main platform points

8. Start getting up to speed on Florida politics

9. Review potential contract with Bryan

10. Purge social media of anything potentially bad

11. Set up dedicated campaign social media accounts

12. Meet Bryan for first campaign photos

13. Break the news to my family that I was running for office

That last one was going to be tricky. My sister would be absolutely supportive, she had been my entire life, but my parents were going to be a whole different story. My folks were some of the staunchest, far-right Republicans I knew, and the only thing worse than getting involved in politics (beyond voting or yelling at the TV), was getting involved in politics as a Democrat. On second thought, I decided that last item on the list could stand to wait for a while.

Updating my voter registration was easy enough. It was a simple matter of finding our county's Supervisor of Elections website and filling out a form. Check one item off the list. The rest of the tasks were a bit more involved, and would take a little bit of time, which was fine. I had just under three weeks until our planned filing date, and most of the list wouldn't be needed for the first month or two anyway.

The next tangible step was meeting Bryan at the county's Democratic Executive Committee meeting, and to start getting to know the local politicos. Since Bryan was a long-time member of the DEC, he was going to wait to make any announcements until the end of the meeting when the floor was opened for that purpose. Most of the meeting would give Christie and I an incognito chance to get a basic lay of the land before we joined the greater county campaign effort. Easy, right?

Being our first political event, and with no guidance to go on, Christie and I again thought it would be smart to dress up a bit. Candidates should look the part, so we rolled up to a dingy, brick community building in the Florida humidity with Christie in a mid-length dress, and me wearing a suit (minus the tie - très Floridian). We were vastly overdressed to say the least, especially when we arrived (again, per usual) about 20 minutes early, well before the DEC was even allowed in the room, since they only had it reserved from 6 p.m. to 8 p.m. The other early arrivals (mostly in jeans and t-shirts) were all milling about outside, chatting in small groups. We stood off by ourselves a bit since we knew exactly zero people there, and Bryan was his usual 15 minutes late.

When the doors finally opened, as "visitors" we were marshalled over to a small sign-in table. We were trying to keep our reason for being there are generic as possible. The volunteer taking our information was very welcoming, and she told us there was a presentation that night.

"The Supervisor of Elections himself is coming tonight," she said excitedly. "He's speaking right after the normal committee business."

Christie and I filed in and grabbed seats near the back of the room. We wanted a good view of how things were run and who the players were. Somewhat surprisingly, we were probably the youngest people in the room by a pretty good margin, but the overall group was represented by a very diverse demographic. Candidates and activists were handing out flyers and business cards while the rest of the attendees found their own seats.

The meeting finally started, and they followed their agenda fairly well, even keeping to Robert's Rules of Order to maintain parliamentary procedures. Nice touch, even if half of the comments and arguments were about the interpretation of Robert's Rules. We listened to everything as the meeting ground on. Truthfully, in my opinion, there was a lot of extraneous chatter and business that probably should have been left to smaller committees, but since this was our very first meeting, who were we to judge?

When the scheduled business was done, the Supervisor of Elections (SoE) was recognized to talk about election security and procedures. He did an excellent job describing the process and answering every question thrown at him. He clarified quite a few things for me, going into the specific procedures that were used in our county which my own election would be subject to. It looked like we picked a good first meeting to attend as it was worth it just for the SoE's presentation. When he finished, the county party chairwoman said that the reserved time was up and another group had the room next, so if there were any announcements, to make them fast. It was Bryan's time to shine, and he jumped up.

"We've found someone to run against Ronda Storms in House District 59! His name is Adam Hattersley, he's a rocket scientist, a veteran, and a Bronze Star recipient! Adam, stand up!" he shouted. And after a beat, the room went nuts! Hearing Ronda's name certainly got everyone's attention, anyone who was remotely political in the county knew her background, and now they were all interested in seeing who was going to run against her.

I stood up and gave a small wave and was promptly swamped by people. What the hell just happened?! Questions came at me from all sides.

"What's your background?"

"What do you want to do in the State House?"

"What do you think about legalizing marijuana?"

"Who's working on your campaign?"

"What issues are you running on?"

"Do you have any campaign literature?"

"Do you need volunteers?"

I could barely discern the different voices, let alone answer any questions (which was good, because besides the background question, I didn't have any answers yet). Over the din around me at the back of the room, the DEC chairwoman was trying to get everyone's attention. It was time to vacate the room for another group. She was getting close to shouting at everyone to get out, when one of the people around me said in a loud voice that they were going to a nearby pub for post-meeting drinks with the Progressive Caucus (the farther left part of the party), and wanted as many people as possible to be there – including Christie and I.

We agreed to meet at the pub and once outside, I was surrounded by a ton of people introducing themselves until Bryan pulled me away.

"That went well," Bryan said with a smile.

"I guess. A bit overwhelming after that boring-ass meeting, though," I said. "We're going to head over to meet people at the bar for drinks."

Different Types of Support

"That's a good idea, get them on board and ready to donate to the campaign. FYI, the people who show up to these meetings are more on the activist/volunteer side of politics, and not as much on the campaign donation side, so don't expect too much," he warned us. "Oh, and before you go, I have a hard copy of the General Consultant contract if you want to give it a last look over and sign it."

I'd read through the draft contract already, and Bryan and I had agreed on a few small changes (which were already in there), so we walked across the parking lot and signed the contract on the trunk of his car. Politics in action.

After the "dark parking lot contract," Christie and I headed over to the bar where we were meeting for after-politics drinks and to talk about – you guessed it – politics. It was a relatively small place about a mile from the meeting site called The Brix, in lovely Ybor City. Ybor is a small section of Tampa known for Cuban cigars, bars, and local history – a "happening" part of town.

We recognized one person at the bar when we arrived. She said that the group would be arriving soon, and she had reserved some tables in the back. She was expecting about 20 people, including the county party chairwoman and at least two other candidates running for the school board. We ordered some drinks and headed back to the tables, not really sure of what to expect for the rest of the evening.

It turned out that most of the discussion was focused on the Progressive's discontent with the county and state party leadership. They all knew (far more than I did at the time) that as Democrats, we had been getting our asses kicked in the state of Florida for a long, long time. The State House had flipped to Republican control over 20 years prior, with the State Senate and Governor's Mansion all shifting to conservatives soon after. The Republican party had held a monopoly on Florida's legislative policy for two full decades, even though there were more registered Democratic voters in the state by a healthy margin. With their majority, the Republicans controlled what the district lines looked like (known as "gerrymandering" where politicians pick their voters instead of voters picking their politicians), and they had padded their lead considerably. The group around the table felt that our party's leadership had taken a too-moderate stance year after year, and without a major change in direction, nothing would change in the state's government.

Christie and I watched and listened with very little idea about what was happening. We were still confused regarding how the party worked (or tried to work or was supposed to work) – which went a long way toward explaining why they had failed election cycle after election cycle. We had to figure out where they went wrong in our small corner of Florida or we would be dead even before leaving the gate.

Adam's fundraising total: $0

Joe's fundraising total: $30,562

Ronda's fundraising total: $1,750

CHAPTER FOUR

The AG's Kickoff Party

Adam and Christie at Sean Shaw's AG kickoff party
Photo used with courtesy of the Hattersley Family

Chapter 4:

The AG's Kickoff Party

March 24, 2018 was my 40th birthday, which fell just about a week after that first confusing county party meeting. My luck, another event was planned for the exact date. I don't know about you, but I really didn't want to spend my 40th at a political to-do surrounded by people I'd never met, few of whom had a clue who I was or had ever heard my name before. But that's exactly where my wife and I wound up. The event was being held at Alex Sink's home. She was the former Chief Financial Officer of Florida and the last Democrat to win a statewide election. Keep in mind, at this point, I'd never spoken to (let alone met) an elected official before.

This particular fete was the campaign kickoff event for Sean Shaw's run for Florida's Attorney General. A campaign kickoff serves two practical purposes:

1) it's a fundraiser (which is the underlying purpose of almost every political event), and

2) it's a splashy way to announce to the world that you're running for office.

The kickoff doesn't have to be the first official campaign activity, it can happen any time once a candidate has opened a campaign bank account. In fact, a campaign can have multiple kickoff events depending how long the campaign has been running and how large a geographic area the office covers. Generally speaking though, the bigger the party (and the more money you raise), the better early indication of support and excitement a candidate can expect.

Back to the story...

We drove to Alex's house on that bright and sunny Spring afternoon. As we got closer, we couldn't believe where we were headed. Even though government officials seem like they are so unreachable and on a whole different planet, the political structure is really a lot flatter than people realize. Once a declared candidate, there are very few levels between you and your Congressman, and you're suddenly rubbing elbows with people you have only previously seen on TV. That said, I was incredibly intimidated and nervous. Those feelings of apprehension grew as we finally found the unmarked dirt road we were looking for and turned onto the property. There was no house in sight.

"Are we in the right place?" Christie asked.

"I hope so," I replied.

Just then we crested a small rise in the road and Alex's house came into view.

There stood the massive, Charleston-style house, a gleaming white structure with wrap-around porches and a few out-buildings, all situated on a beautiful Central Florida lake. The house was centered on nearly 12 acres, about two of which were reserved for dry scrub grass, which was functioning as a makeshift parking lot where nearly 100 cars were already parked.

"Yup, this is the place," I said as I rolled down my window to take directions from the parking attendant (yes, there was a parking attendant, several, in fact).

We parked amidst the sea of grass and cars and just sat still for a minute. Were we really ready for this? We had felt out of our depth at a relatively casual party meeting just the week prior. More importantly (and as we had asked ourselves several times since deciding to run), what had we gotten ourselves into?

"Our first priority is to find Bryan," Christie said.

I couldn't agree more. Although still a relatively new acquaintance to us, compared to a house full of strangers, he was like an old friend, and his would be the only face we would recognize besides politicians we had previously only seen on TV.

I pulled on my sport coat as Christie and I headed to the house. It was a "Florida warm" day (meaning mid-80s and humid, in other words, hot as hell anywhere else), so wearing a jacket really didn't help my comfort level. Maybe my first priority would be finding some water.

As we got closer to the house, we realized new arrivals were congregating at a small check-in table. This was where they could sign in (participation credit!) and leave a donation either via Sean's website that was open on a laptop and manned by a volunteer or by dropping a check into a large bowl. Besides raising all important campaign dollars, the volunteers were capturing every attendee's mailing and email addresses. I would soon learn that having a robust contact list is also vitally important in any political campaign. The larger the list, the more people the campaign can communicate with about issues, volunteer opportunities, and of course, ask for additional campaign donations.

Check in and donation completed, we quickly found Bryan and he immediately introduced us to anyone and everyone who would give us the time of day. Unfortunately, that was fewer people than we were hoping for. I was a bit surprised to learn that nearly half the people attending the party were political candidates themselves. Little did I know that the same people consistently showed up to these events because if you are a candidate, attendance is practically mandatory. We met people running for City Council, the School Board, the County Commission, multiple state House and Senate seats, as well as the man himself, Sean Shaw, running statewide for Attorney General.

One very important person we met was a current State Representative, running for reelection, and an old friend of Bryan's. Ben Diamond represented Florida's House District 68 in St. Petersburg, and was a lawyer in his own firm. He was close to my age, in his early 40s, had dark hair and was slightly overweight, with a very welcoming face. Ben was one of the first actual elected officials I had ever met and I was impressed that he took time to talk to me.

"Adam Hattersley? I just heard your name last week; you're going to be running in District 59?" Ben asked.

Wait a minute, an elected official had heard my name? How did that happen? Bryan answered that question straight off.

"He is! This is the guy I called you about the other day, Ben," Bryan said.

That was part of what being a political consultant was – making sure donors and elected officials knew who his clients were and getting those people to support his clients. "He's our best shot at this seat in a long time, but we're definitely going to need your help raising some money."

"How did we do in that district last election?" Ben asked.

"Not so great," Bryan told him. "Lost by nine points, but it was against a two-time incumbent. The good news, though, is that the incumbent isn't running for re-election, so now it's an open seat."

"That is good! Statistically, incumbents have an 85% chance of winning, so an open seat definitely increases your odds," he said, turning to me and then back to Bryan. "That was Spano, right? Yeah, he was tough to beat, and if I remember, we had a really good candidate, too. Raised some solid money."

"We did, but the Presidential year was rough in that part of the county," Bryan answered. Bryan didn't particularly need me around for this conversation (I was still a bit out of my depth, anyway), but I stood there nodding my head feeling like an idiot all the same.

"Well, give me a call in a few weeks and I'll see what I can do to help out," Ben said, shifting his attention to me. "Bryan has my number. I have to go; I'm introducing Sean in a few minutes."

Introducing Sean? This being my first political fundraiser, I wasn't sure what to expect, but I should have known the candidate would address the group. I would soon learn that these events had a pretty standard agenda. Typically, someone acted as the emcee, who may or may not also be the first speaker (in this case, it was Alex Sink herself, which made sense since we were all at her home). The emcee generally then turns the stage over to the warm-up speaker, someone who knows the candidate well (a co-worker, another elected official, or even a significant other) to talk the candidate up and give them more legitimacy. That person will usually pass the stage to the candidate themself to make a rousing speech to convince everyone present that they, and no one else, are the only one who could possibly win. Now, the last speaker (frequently the warm-up person) comes back one last time for perhaps the most important part of the event – "the ask." Even though most, if not all, of the people at the event have already donated to the candidate's campaign, the ask implores them to double down on their financial support. The ask can be sympathetic, spirited or challenging as long as it doesn't sound too desperate.

Alex appeared on her raised patio with a microphone and let everyone know that "the show" was about to begin. She gave a quick overview of how the election season (like football season, elections absolutely have a season) was shaping up in Florida, and of course, praised the candidate we were all there to see – State Representative Sean Shaw. Alex talked about how getting Sean elected to Attorney General – and if we could also elect a Democrat to the Governor's Mansion – that would be all the (current) minority party (the Democrats) in the state would need to make all state cabinet decisions. A very big deal. She also spoke about how down ballot races could go a long way in helping the larger statewide races find success.

Alex paused while everyone in the crowd nodded their heads in agreement, and then she asked every other candidate present to say their name, what they were running for, and who their opponent was. Since Bryan made the announcement at the DEC meeting the previous week, this would be the first time I actually said anything myself in front of a political gathering. Immediately, my nerves kicked in. I watched a few other candidates go first giving myself the chance to hear examples of what to say.

"Hi! I'm Fentrice Driskell, running in State House District 63 against Shawn Harrison," a tall woman yelled out from the other side of the gathering. People clapped and there were a few shouts of support.

"I'm Deb Bellanti, running in House District 60!" another woman announced and received a similar reaction.

Bryan leaned over to whisper to me. "Make sure you say you're running against Ronda Storms," he said. "Trust me."

The crowd made the familiar approvals as the next two candidates introduced themselves. I decided I was ready to take my turn so I piped up, "I'm Adam Hattersley, I will be running in House District 59!" I shouted. I was received by the same subdued but positive reaction as everyone else. Then I added, "I'm running against Ronda Storms!"

The crowd went nuts!!

This group was deep Florida politics, and they all knew about Ronda's exploits. In fact, a couple of people were present who had served with her in both the Legislature and the County Commission, people I absolutely needed to get introduced to. Bryan gave a little. "I told you to say that" smirk, and Christie was beaming by my side.

"Now *that's* a race we need to make sure to win!" Alex said into the microphone, prompting another cheer. *What the hell just happened?* People standing near me began introducing themselves: a former president of the Florida Justice Association, a County Commissioner, and the past President of the University of South Florida. (Did I mention this party was packed with the "it" crowd of Central Florida politics?) It was overwhelming. Luckily, Alex kept the program moving and regained the group's attention. My head was swimming with so many new names and faces, I hardly remembered the rest of the speakers. But fortunately, after the formal program was over, the fun meet-and-greet portion of the event allowed Christie and I to meet one more important person.

Let me talk a bit more about the hostess of this upper-class political shindig. Alex Sink was the last Democrat elected statewide in Florida, serving as the Chief Financial Officer. She was also the Democratic party's nominee for Governor in 2010. My wife Christie had seen her speak years before at a *Women in Business* event in Tampa and had been enamored with her ever since. For over a decade, she was seen as the matriarch of Florida Democratic politics. Needless to say, Christie was excited to meet Alex, and we saw our chance as the event wound down.

"There she is!" Christie exclaimed, pointing to a petite woman with short dark hair standing on the porch with a small crowd around her. "Bryan, can you introduce us?"

"Sure, let's work our way over. I've known Alex for ages," he suggested.

Alex had a warm smile on her face as we approached with Christie eagerly marshalling us along. "Oh, Hi Bryan!" she said.

"Hey, Alex! Great job with this event. I want to introduce you to Adam and Christie Hattersley. He's the one running against Ronda Storms in District 59," Bryan said while making room so we could shake Alex's hand.

"It's great to meet you!" Christie jumped in. "I saw you speak a few years ago, and sorry to fangirl, but I think you're great!"

"So sweet of you! Bryan, tell me more about your client."

"Before that, I need to talk to you about getting early support for my County Commission candidate," Bryan began. Both Alex's, and Christie's faces dropped, but for very different reasons. Alex knew that Bryan was about to attempt to pressure her into something that she had no intention of doing, so she immediately went into work mode. Christie knew that our opportunity for conversation was now gone, so she and I went into forced spectator mode. Bryan and Alex whisper-argued for about five minutes, then Alex, seeming to have had enough, announced that she had to speak to someone (anyone, probably) and promptly dismissed us.

Christie was visibly disappointed. For days, she had been waiting excitedly, like a kid before Christmas, to meet Alex Sink and that was the interaction we got. Do keep in mind, though, that every other time I've spoken to Alex since, she has been one of the nicest, brightest people I've ever met. We just caught her during a bad (and somewhat hijacked) conversation.

We waded back into the crowd and found ourselves near Ben Diamond again, who was chatting with the man of the hour himself, Sean Shaw. The two of them had been lawyers on Alex's staff at the Capitol and now were both first-term State Representatives. Sean is a genuinely optimistic guy, and with his six-foot six-inch frame, has the presence of a linebacker.

Ben introduced me, and Sean's voice boomed out, "So! You're the guy running against Ronda, huh? I'm going to need your help in that district. What do you think your chances are?"

I had no idea what my chances were. Even in politics though, that type of situation calls for a "fake it until you make it" approach. "I think we have a shot. I'm certainly going to do the best I can," I said. Seemed like a good non-committal yet rosy answer.

"That's great. Let me know what I can do to help," Sean said. In reality, that was probably what he said to everyone he didn't know, but with a couple hundred people at his party, I absolutely understood his response.

As the event was starting to wind down, I told Bryan that it was time to go. Christie and I had dinner reservations that night at a swanky Tampa restaurant for my birthday, and if we wanted to make it on time, we needed to leave. We said our good byes and got a few more well-wishes from new acquaintances. Bryan assured me that the newborn Hattersley Campaign made some very positive first impressions. We felt good as we drove to dinner.

I might have ended this part of my story here, but something happened at dinner, or rather before dinner that's definitely worth mentioning. Christie had made reservations at a great Tampa fixture of a restaurant call Donatello's. It has a "Rat Pack" 1950s vibe, impeccable service, and is the only place to get Lobster Thermidor (a personal and expensive favorite reserved for birthday celebrations and special occasions) in town. We got there about 10 minutes before our reservation, so we headed to the bar to grab a glass of wine.

Next to us was an elegant couple that looked to be in their mid-60s, also enjoying a pre-dinner drink and the dimly lit atmosphere. They were (in all likelihood) a couple of glasses of wine ahead of us, when the woman noticed us.

"Good evening!" she cheerily said to get our attention. "What brings you two here tonight?"

"It's my husband's birthday!" Christie replied.

"Oh, that's wonderful! Happy birthday! Did you do anything special today?"

"Well, we went to our very first political event. We're starting to get involved locally" I told her.

"Splendid! I've been involved in politics myself for several years! What do you plan on doing?" she asked (a bit in her cups and seemingly in a good mood).

"Actually, I'm going to be running for the Florida House of Representatives," I said. "On the East side of town in the Brandon area."

"That's lovely! I was the president of a county Republican Party here for several years in the 1990s. I'm sure I could connect you with Republican groups and churches out that way," she was nearly beaming at this point, but Christie's face fell a little (a lot, to be honest). "We absolutely need more young Christian conservatives legislating by the gospel in Tallahassee."

"Well, um... I'm actually running as a Democrat," I told her.

Her mood darkened quicker than a fastball. "Oh. Well. You should look at what the Bible says about those gays and how unnatural they are. Even a *Democrat* can understand *that*," she nearly snarled, making sure to emphasize words that seemed difficult for her to say. "You seem like a nice young man, and I'll pray for you to see the error of your ways, but I hope you lose," she continued as she got up and nearly dragged her companion away from us and across the room.

I was shocked. Christie was shocked. *What the hell just happened?* Is this the kind of reception we should expect from everyone based on a political party name associated with our nascent campaign? This woman went from happily helpful to aggressively vitriolic in a matter of seconds. I knew politics divided people, but I never knew to what extent, especially based on nothing more than party label.

I couldn't stop thinking about how little I knew about this new world I was stepping into as Christie and I followed the host to our table. What had we gotten ourselves into? The day had started so full of positive energy and then we run into... wow... *whatever that was* at the bar. I was quickly learning that not only did I need to grow a thicker skin, but also a shorter memory when it came to conversations like that one. It was *my* birthday after all, and I would be damned if I would let *that* woman ruin it.

There were a lot of lessons from the day. Candidates are going to run into more types of people than they can possibly imagine during a campaign (or even before one officially starts). You will meet good people and bad people during the process, people who want to help and people who would rather hinder. You must be willing to learn from all of them – either things to do, or things not to do. Ways to treat people, and ways to not treat people. Take advantage of every meeting and interaction. Learn as much as you can. Take everything with a grain of salt. It makes you a stronger candidate.

Adam's fundraising total: $0

Joe's fundraising total: $33,037

Ronda's fundraising total: $3,550

CHAPTER FIVE

Welcome to Chaos

Adam at a labor union BBQ
Photo used with courtesy of the Hattersley Family

Chapter 5:

Welcome to Chaos

I'm going to offer a quick primer for this chapter because things may seem a bit chaotic and all over the place. There's a reason for that. The pace of a campaign and the life of a candidate can frequently be what we call in the biz, "a shit show." Events and meetings will overlap and time in the car traveling from one venue to the next will pile up. Juggling the things you *should* attend with the things you *can* attend, not to mention maintaining your private life, becomes an intricate dance. Prioritizing importance is key, but don't ignore the smaller events just because they are small. Anyway... on with our regularly scheduled programming.

Meetings and Calls

Now that our decision was made and my candidacy was public, there was some paperwork to finalize. We were in the last few days of March and had decided that the official filing date for the campaign would be April 2nd – a Monday. We figured this would give me the most time to show a strong fundraising month. Coincidentally, one of Bryan's other clients, Kim Overman, was having her kickoff event that very evening. Like all the other candidates within a 20-mile radius, I was expected to be at the event. So, Bryan and I planned to sign the filing papers at that event. He had everything printed and filled out; all I had to do was sign my name on the dotted line.

Christie and I arrived at the party a little late this time and Kim was already giving her speech as we arrived. She was starting to recognize other candidates and by chance said my name just as I was coming through the door. I waved (maybe a little too meekly) as we made our way across the room. I quickly scanned the room and the other attendees' faces. Besides Bryan, who was serving as the event's emcee, I recognized only a few other people there – political candidates all.

The event went off without a hitch, and as it wound down, Bryan popped over to let me know he had the filing documents in his car. We walked across the street to sign them in what may be one of the least ceremonious fashions. I signed the three required documents while leaning on a car trunk in a parking lot just after sunset. Perhaps the easiest part of running for political office was now complete with no fanfare whatsoever.

Over the next few days, things moved in strange spurts of activity, followed by excruciating delays. I did my best to begin the process of setting up the financial part of my new campaign. Bright and early that Tuesday morning, I opened an account at the bank declared on my filing forms and began the process of integrating it with the online fundraising platform we had chosen. Here's where the waiting came into play which was frustrating since I needed to start raising money, and the easiest way for people to donate was online. The fundraising platform took up to seven days to verify a person's candidacy and banking information. *Shit! I wish I had known that seven days ago.*

Luckily, and to Bryan's chagrin, I had something else to focus on. I've mentioned earlier that I was a gymnastics official, but it's actually a little more complicated than that. For the 2018 and 2019 competitive seasons, I was serving as one of the six National Apparatus Leaders for the U.S. Junior Program. That meant that I had agreed to be the head judge at the U.S. Junior National Championships for the next two years. That came with several other obligations – things I had committed to do over a year ago – and by God, I was going to live up to those commitments. Beyond the National Championships, I was also scheduled to judge several large regional meets, and that Thursday, April 5th, I was flying to Boston to judge a large, multi-state competition.

Since my newly established campaign was in a temporary time out while waiting for our finances to be established, Bryan wasn't too broken up about me leaving for four days, as long as I promised to ask all my gym buddies to contribute to the campaign while I was away. Easy compromise. As a side note, the competition went swimmingly well, and on the last day (Sunday), my fundraising platform finally turned on and I received my very first contribution. It was a great feeling, even though it was only $100, and by the end of that day, four of my gym friends had grown my Day One haul to $500. *Score!*

I flew home feeling good about the weekend. I had a packed schedule for my truncated week ahead since I was leaving for another gymnastics competition in Georgia that Thursday. I had one main task before I left, to begin the months-long process of getting comfortable with call time.

Call time is a candidate's bread and butter. Call time fuels a campaign. *Call time is a giant pain in the ass.* It's horrible. Basically, a candidate will dial someone (friend, family member or most often, a stranger) and – for lack of a better term – "beg" them for money. It's how a campaign survives and raises the money it needs to do all the other, more forward-facing, campaign-related things. One of the first steps though, even before a maiden voyage "dialing for dollars" session, is something called "rolodexing."

For you younger folks, a rolodex was an office tool similar to your cell phone's contact list. It was a circular file card-holding device where, you guessed it, a person kept all their contact information. In the olden days, a candidate would start at the first 'A' entry in their rolodex and call that person. When that call was done, you flip the card to the second entry and dial that number, and so on and so on until you got through everyone in your rolodex. Simple, right? Today's world isn't all that different, except a candidate can now export all of their contact info (not just from your phone, but also from all of your various social media accounts) into a consolidated spreadsheet. This is where you keep notes, dates, conversation details, relationships, and information about how large of a contribution you're requesting, and more. For better funded campaigns, which by the way, I was not, you can purchase auto-dialer software to increase calling speed and efficiency. Basically, rolodexing is consolidating your potential donor information, prioritizing who to call and what to ask.

Once that fun trip down memory lane was finished (I had fond memories of almost everyone on my list), the next step was coming up with a solid script. This is more important when calling strangers, but it's good to have it to refer back to even when you're talking to friends. A good script should be relatively short and consist of a few things:

- A brief introduction and why you're calling
- Why you're running and why you want to serve
- Why you're the best candidate
- How you will win, and
- What you need from them

That last part is extremely important. You're asking people to invest in you and your campaign, and no one wants to waste their money on someone who doesn't have a plan to win. Why are you different from past candidates? What makes *this* election's conditions better than the last? What is your path to victory, and how can the person you are talking to help you get there? Sounds easy, right? On paper sure; in practice, not so much.

By the time I finished rolodexing (and a little bit of procrastination), it was time to head to Georgia for the gymnastics competition. It was about a four-hour drive, and another judge-buddy of mine was in the driver's seat. That meant I was free to start making actual phone calls. Something I forgot to mention, call time is also extremely awkward, especially for a rookie like me. It becomes doubly awkward when there is an audience present. It becomes triply awkward when your first list comes from your consultant and is full of people you've never met but who have a history of supporting local Democrats. My heart rate was already elevated before I dialed the first number.

As I said, call time is horrible and now, even worse, I was making those calls from a moving vehicle. I'm not normally a glutton for punishment, but there I was, embarking on my first attempt at call time, full of optimism that I would rake in hundreds (if not thousands) of dollars while driving to Georgia.

I could not have been more wrong.

My first call went to voicemail, which confirmed that, at least, I had the correct phone number. I left a message. Okay. The second call was a disconnected number. The third and fourth both went to voicemail. The fifth person hung up on me mid-introduction, but at least it was someone alive on the other end of the line. Six more voicemails before another living person who told me that I had no chance and that they weren't going to waste their money on a loser. My driving companion was starting to eye me curiously at this point.

I think you get the idea how this first calling session went, and after two hours and over 50 numbers dialed, I was exactly zero dollars better funded and completely dispirited. My "connect rate" (percentage of pickups compared to number of dials) was less than eight percent – which is terrible – and my "hit rate" (number of donations compared to number of dials) was zero. My travelling buddy looked at me with sympathy and simply said, "That was the worst thing I've ever had to listen to in my life." After that disaster, we decided to sit in silence for the rest of the ride, which was probably a merciful decision for both of us. Not a very auspicious fundraising start, to say the least.

The gymnastics weekend, however, was a fun one. I got a few people to make some very small donations to the campaign, but at this point, every contribution felt like a big victory, so I was happy. The ride home after the competition was much better, too, since my buddy made me promise there would be no phone calls from the car. I'm not sure which of us was more pleased by that request.

The following week promised to be busy. Besides call time during work hours, I made my first appearances at local Democratic clubs and caucus meetings. For most of these events, my wife, Christie, came with me. She is my secret weapon. She can talk to anyone, all the while making them feel as comfortable as possible. She knows how to work a room better than any other person I know, and I tried my best to learn her methods because I was sure I would be fielding questions and meeting hundreds of new people all over the Tampa Bay area. Starting with the clubs affiliated with my own party was a way to ease into the political world with little risk since they would all (hopefully) be supportive.

The first meeting I attended was the East Hillsborough County Democratic Club, which was the local Dem club in my neck of the woods. These folks were the core Democrats in my district, and would, with any luck, play an important role in my campaign. They met at a local pub, usually over chicken wings and beer, nice and casual and a great way to break in a new candidate.

A lot of the clubs and caucuses have overlapping membership, and the East Hillsborough Dems were no different. Several of their members had been at the DEC meeting a few weeks prior and had heard Bryan announce my candidacy. Most of them had lived in the area for decades and were well versed in the Republican candidates' platforms, so I was greeted with enthusiastic cheers when I arrived. Not a bad way to start! It turns out, the president of the club had run for the very seat that I was now vying for four years ago. She was a person I would need to get to know since she had a much better understanding of the local political landscape.

The meeting went smoothly, and I was given a few minutes to introduce myself and talk about why I was running. I'm glad I started with this group since they were already knowledgeable. Christie made some new friends, and we got contact info for people wanting to volunteer for door knocking (something I would have to learn about since I didn't quite know what that meant). All in all, it was a good night, including the moderately satisfying chicken wings.

The next day was a little more hectic. After call time (of course), we headed to our first meetings of the Hillsborough Disability Caucus and the county LGBTQ Caucus, which were held in the same location one right after the other, so no extra travel time required. I needed to diligently court these groups, especially since one of my opponents was so anti-LGBTQ, and defending those rights was one of my cornerstones for running. Not to mention the head of the county's Disability Caucus was also the president of the statewide organization, so seeing her on a regular basis would go a long way to getting the larger group's support. Again, warm welcomes all around and info for more campaign volunteers.

The following day, there were more new meetings on my schedule. We started at the county's Sierra Club branch, where one member's solution to every environmental problem in the land was to "plant more palmetto trees." I'm sure she had her reasons. Then, we hurried over to the already-in-progress Young Democrats meeting. We met up with several other candidates there, after which we scurried back across town to catch the tail end of the East County Women's Club meeting. One night, two hours, 120 miles in the car and three political meetings. This, folks, is a candidate's typical agenda. Pace yourself but be ready to be busy.

This early chaos brings up an interesting thing; if possible, have a campaign surrogate (or two). A surrogate is someone you trust who knows you well and can speak about your platform on your behalf. Having a surrogate allows your campaign to be at more than one place at a time to get in front of more people. My surrogate was, of course, Christie. If I was stuck someplace, she would stand in for me somewhere else. If it was a big event, we would each go our separate ways to engage more people and hopefully double our effectiveness. But I digress.

When running for office, your days are no longer typical. The trick is to put yourself out there, makes friends and allies, listen, and of course, *be everywhere*. These early weeks further enforced my initial thoughts about running for office. *What the hell did I get myself into?*

Adam's fundraising total: $3,590

Joe's fundraising total: $33,737

Ronda's fundraising total: $4,150

CHAPTER SIX

The Endorsement Process

Adam speaking to the East Hillsborough Democratic Club
Photo used with courtesy of the Hattersley Family

Chapter 6:

The Endorsement Process

By connecting with people closest to us, the first few weeks of fundraising went surprisingly well. My in-laws and friends were pleasantly generous and at the same time, I learned about additional important parts of a campaign – endorsement questionnaires and interviews. Have you ever wondered how that comes about when you see a political commercial or advertisement that touts, "Endorsed by XYZ"? Each group has its own process. Some are simple, and some are not simple. Different "perks" if you will, can come with endorsements. Some come with campaign contributions, some with recommendations to their membership, some give volunteers, and some offer a combination. Endorsements can be a bothersome process, but there are definite reasons to pursue them.

Let's start with a simple one. I've mentioned going to the county LGBTQ Caucus meeting. They also endorse candidates. For many groups, getting a county endorsement is the first step in getting statewide endorsement, and the LGBTQ Caucus followed that path. Since I was the only Democrat in my race, all I needed to get their endorsement was fill out a simple yes/no questionnaire and voilà! I received an email of my endorsement (which was great, since most of my active volunteers came from this group).

A quick note about these questionnaires; one of the first questions is always, "How much money have you raised?" This is a benchmark question. This measurable indicator of a campaign is used to assess "candidate viability," a fancy way of saying "Is this person working hard, do they stand a chance in this contest, and do they deserve my support?" *Everyone* asks this question. Organizations, reporters, donors ... everyone. It's a bit of a vicious cycle, though. Groups and donors don't want to waste their time supporting a non-viable candidate, which makes it even harder on those campaigns to raise money. Conversely, people (and money) flock to a candidate that is already raising strong campaign cash, which turns into attention and then even more resources. The more money you raise, the more people are inclined to donate, and the less you raise, the less chance you have of gaining donors. Good cycles and bad cycles.

And now for an example of a not-so-simple endorsement process – the Florida Chamber of Commerce. Traditionally, Chambers of Commerce are conservative and rarely endorse a Democrat in a contested race. But going after the endorsement at least gave us a chance to get to know each other and based on the three people currently in my race, I was (naïvely) hopeful.

The Chamber's process started, like many others, with a questionnaire. This questionnaire, however, was 57 essay questions long. I am 100% serious. Questions ranged the gamut from simple candidate biography stuff to in-depth positions on minute economic policies. These questions required research and knowledge of current Florida statutes and a description of the candidate's plans for the future of the state's economy. I spent a couple weeks on this thing, and still wasn't finished when my wife and I spent a weekend in New Orleans with my family. In a mild panic, I planned to finish and submit the questionnaire on our last day away (a Sunday) – one day before it was due.

Sunday morning rolled around, and I had already warned my parents that I would be holed up in my hotel room until my homework was complete. Luckily, my secret weapon (Christie) was there to help me. We spent over four hours putting the finishing touches on more than three weeks of work to get everything just right before hitting the "send" button on the questionnaire. And believe it or not, that was less than half the battle.

The following week, I drove about 90 minutes to a hotel just outside Disney World for the interview portion of the Chamber's endorsement process. This was no ordinary one-on-one interview, mind you, but the largest panel interview I had ever seen. There were close to 100 prominent members of the Florida Chamber of Commerce, from all walks of business life, arranged in a giant horseshoe in the hotel's largest conference room. One small table sat at the mouth of the horseshoe with a glass of water and a microphone on it; that was where I was supposed to sit. Oh, and did I mention this was my *first* candidate interview? Talk about nervous!

When my turn came, and I was (relatively) comfortable in the "hot seat," the panel's moderator explained that I was one of over 80 candidates they were seeing that week for endorsement consideration (and yes, they had already spoken with the two Republicans in my race). I had two minutes to introduce myself, then the panel had 15-20 minutes to ask me anything. *Anything.* Items from the questionnaire, thoughts that popped into their heads, literally anything. I took a sip of water to try and calm my rattled nerves before launching into my bio.

Their inquisition was, shall I say, vigorous. It seemed like I had a couple of allies in the room, but not many. The discussion was lively, and a couple of my answers solicited some intended laughs, so a little of my personality came through. Overall, I got a fairly warm reception, and I was feeling good about the whole thing. A few of the panelists (my suspected allies) followed me out of the room when I was finished to chat further. They told me that they liked me far better than my opponents, but since I was a Democrat, I flatly had no chance of getting the endorsement whatsoever. I no longer felt good about the whole thing. I thanked them for their frankness, exchanged contact information, and headed to my car to stew during the long drive home. Back in the depths of my mind, I knew that simply going through the process was worth it to get my name in front of more people, but it was hard not to feel like I had wasted my time.

After the "How much cash have you raised" question, endorsement interviews also usually ask why a person is running for public office. This can be a tricky question and can absolutely reveal what type of elected official a candidate will be. I was gearing up for another endorsement interview with the Associated Builders and Contractors (ABC) which was involved, but not as much as the Florida Chamber's process. The ABC is another group known to support more conservative candidates. Sometimes a c⁻ ʼate has to be a glutton for punishment.

ʼɔomy, rainy day when I arrived at their building ᶠ downtown Tampa, and as usual, I was about ʼrly. The receptionist told me they had two other candidates scheduled before me, so I settled in to wait in their front office. I was rehearsing answers in my head and watching the rain when a beautiful $250,000 white Bentley Continental Coupe glided into the parking lot. It parked next to my car (shaming my modest little Kia) and a statuesque blonde woman emerged and strode to the door of the ABC Building. She checked in with the clerk, who told her she was just in time for her interview, but would need to wait a few minutes before she was up. She sat down across from me and started chatting.

"Hi. Are you here for the candidate interviews, too?" she asked.

"Yes. Very nice to meet you! Where are you running?"

"A bit south of here. I just got so fed up with having to pay infrastructure fees when I build and sell new homes and buildings, while the old people who move down here from New England that buy them from me don't have to pay the same fees when they sell," she explained. (Side note: the fees she was talking about are one-time impact fees when new construction goes in, mostly to pay for the utilities routed to the building and are enacted everywhere in the country.)

The reason she was running was that ultimately, she personally wanted to be richer. She was already driving a quarter-million-dollar car and selling new buildings all over the place, and she was trying to get into public office to benefit no one but herself and her bank account. *What the hell?*

I didn't even have a chance to respond before she was called in for her interview. She got up and sauntered into the conference room with a flippant "good luck" over her shoulder to me. I was flabbergasted. Our problems with elected officials and government were starting to become clearer to me every day.

Ultimately, each candidate is going to have their own reason(s) to run. Be it personal, economic, idealistic, or foolish; make sure to know your reason. It's a question you'll get asked more than any other, and even if your answer doesn't get you the support or endorsement of the person who asked it, make sure it's the right reason. And a word of warning: stay consistent with your reason. Don't change your answers simply to garner one organization's favor or another's. Politics is a smaller world than people realize and these groups absolutely talk to one another. Inconsistency is a hallmark of indecision, which is never a good trait in a politician. Not to mention it will come back to bite you with a vengeance!

Adam's fundraising total: $6,142

Joe's fundraising total: $33,862

Ronda's fundraising total: $4,150

CHAPTER SEVEN

The Campaign Kickoff

Tahlah Campbell Joseph, Adam, and Sofia Segami at Adam's kickoff party
Photo used with courtesy of the Hattersley Family

Chapter 7:

The Campaign Kickoff

Beyond the fundraising, meetings, and endorsements, there was still one major thing we had to do at the start of our little campaign, and I already had a few examples to go by for my kickoff event. We settled on the last Tuesday in April because it gave us time to plan it and ensured that any money we raised counted toward our first official month of fundraising.

A lot more goes into one of these events than you would realize. Besides settling on a date, we had several tasks ahead of us:

- Find and secure a venue
- Procure a microphone and sound system
- Get at least two volunteers
- Design a campaign logo
- Settle on my slogan
- Design large stand-up signs
- Arrange for food and drinks
- Design and order campaign t-shirts/swag
- Write a compelling stump speech
- Convince people to show up

There was plenty to do, and really that list described only the big-ticket items. Fortunately, my digital guy, Chris Mitchell, was already working on our logo and slogan, and since I was handy with some design programs, it fell to me to work on our signage and swag designs (adding more time-consuming tasks to my already busy schedule of call time, meetings and interviews).

As always, my secret weapon, Christie, was already on point to make sure this event was a success. She was having lunch with a couple of her friends, and they agreed to be our volunteers; all they asked for in return was a campaign t-shirt which, unbeknownst to them, we had planned to force on them anyway. One task officially checked off the list. That lunch just so happened to be at a centrally located little pub, complete with its own microphone, sound system and small stage. Thinking quickly, Christie asked if they ever hosted events, and if they were free on the last Tuesday in April. She chatted with the manager and found out that not only were Tuesdays their slowest day of the week, but the manager was a Democrat! He offered the place up for free, provided we had a cash bar. Done and done! Just like that, Christie had sewed up some of the most difficult items on our to-do list. (I told you she was my secret weapon.)

Venue, sound, and volunteers arranged, I started on my speech. The plan was to come up with a solid, memorable speech that I could use in multiple situations, part introduction, part platform, part motivation for seeking office, and part rah-rah, go Team Adam! Easier said than done. Whenever I had free time between the other campaign and kickoff tasks, I worked on my speech. I must have gone through about a dozen drafts of a simple five-minute speech before I was remotely ready to begin practicing it. Whenever I got frustrated with my speech progress (or lack thereof), I designed more of our campaign swag.

Chris, Bryan, Christie, and I finally decided on a logo after a dozen iterations, for most of our swag items. Luckily, I got the t-shirt order in on time to (barely) make the event. The trickiest part was designing the big stand-up signs. Also called pop-up signs, they are common at trade shows, retail stores, and conferences. They come in a carrying case and are basically a rolled-up vinyl banner in a box that extends to approximately seven feet high. Besides our new logo, these signs also needed a bit more information; two or three points of my platform, some minor biographical data, and the warmest headshot we had. All our swag was, of course, decked out in my campaign colors (also my Alma Mater's colors) of maize and blue. Easy, right?

Things were coming together. We arranged party platter orders at our local grocery store for some snacks, and now all we really had left was getting as many people as possible to the event. About two weeks before our kickoff, I started a little blitz to all our local clubs' social media pages, and the digital team sent out RSVP links. We wanted to get an idea of how many people to expect. Keep in mind that usually only about 60% of those who RSVP actually show up. Our swag and signage started to arrive, and my speech was ... improving? Well, at least Christie told me it was getting better. And she would certainly know after indulging me by listening to me practice it from across the house repeatedly. Beyond the words of the speech, I needed to work on projecting my voice so the people in the back could hear.

Kickoff day arrived and we had everything set except the shirts, which were ready for pick up at a shop about 40 miles away from where we needed them. Bryan jumped in his car and assured us that he would not only pick them up but navigate Tampa rush hour traffic smoothly enough that he would get to the pub on time, and off he went in a screech of tires. If my nerves hadn't already kicked in, they made their appearance after watching Bryan speed out of the parking lot.

Christie and I went in to set up, and after a few minutes, our two volunteers arrived. Of course, the first thing they asked was, "Where are our t-shirts?" They accepted that the shirts would be arriving shortly and set up the check-in table. The table is a pretty simple thing; it has a couple of sign-in sheets to capture everyone's information, a large bowl for people to deposit any checks, and a laptop computer or two set to the campaign's donation website. Stickers or additional swag with the campaign logo (if we could have afforded them) are usually placed near the check-in table.

It was starting to look like a real political event when Bryan, who must have set a land-speed record, came running in, out of breath carrying a box of our t-shirts. The final piece of the puzzle had arrived! The very first Hattersley for State House shirts went to our two intrepid volunteers as promised (Thanks, Tahlah and Sophia!). We had our signs set up, the food out, and sound system tested. We were ready!

We were ready, and alone for the next 20 minutes. Bryan got us a round of beers and told us not to worry, no one showed up to these things on time. I was starting to panic the farther along I got on my beer when, thankfully, about 15 people arrived all at the same time. Christie and I shared a big sigh of relief while people checked in and started focusing on keeping the room's energy as high as possible. Within the next half hour, the pub was full with about 50 people who were excited to help us win. Let me tell you, it was a great feeling.

Just like at Kim's kickoff a few weeks before, Bryan acted as the event's emcee. He spoke briefly about his hopes for a victory come November and passed the mic to Christie. She always does a magnificent and flattering job telling our story. She spoke from the heart, which is a much more engaging way to capture an audience unlike the rote and choppy speech I was about to give (don't worry, I eventually get better at that part). My performance was almost a footnote compared to my wife's, and not particularly memorable. After my somewhat stumbling remarks, Bryan took back control to make the plea for additional campaign donations. After that, it simply turned into a party. Isn't that how the best events end up?

No matter how daunting some of these campaign activities seem to be at first and no matter how clumsy they start out — be it fundraising, endorsements, interviews, or events, they do get easier. And trust me, any candidate is going to get plenty of practice. The key is to keep moving forward. Keep practicing. Don't give up just because something is hard or intimidating. If you want to get into public office, you're going to face difficult situations eventually, so you might as well get good at them as early on as possible.

Adam's fundraising total: $11,877
Joe's fundraising total: $34,546
Ronda's fundraising total: $8,150

CHAPTER EIGHT

Strategizing

Bryan Farris, Christie, Adam, and Chris Mitchell
Photo used with courtesy of the Hattersley Family

Chapter 8:
Strategizing

One old Chief Petty Officer I knew when I was in the Navy used to always say, "Prior Proper Planning Prevents Piss Poor Performance." He called it "the seven Ps." I realize that he didn't originate the alliterative rule, but whenever we were faced with a task, he would simply look at the group and mention "the seven Ps," and how if we followed them, we would be successful.

A political campaign is no different. Having a solid, yet flexible plan early on is key. In fact, it's so critical, it's your roadmap to victory. Without a plan, the candidate and team would flail around, bouncing from activity to activity with no clear direction. I had decided to run for office. I had filed to run for office. Now, I needed a plan on how to win that office.

My General Consultant, Bryan Farris, and his partner-in-politics (and our digital guy) Chris Mitchell, had been working on a comprehensive campaign plan and were ready to review it with me. As the candidate, I had final approval of everything going on with the campaign (it was my name on the ballot, after all, not to mention my signature on the checks that would pay for everything), exactly as it should be. So, the three of us set up a time to meet at a local restaurant to get "down in the weeds" by diving into the details of the proposed plan with a fine-toothed comb.

Like always, I was the first to arrive for our meeting (another Navy saying I try to live by is, "If you're not early, you're late"), so I found us a table on the patio since it was a beautiful, late Spring day. Chris arrived next, very shortly followed by Bryan, who plunked three copies of the campaign plan on the table.

"Here it is!" he proudly said. "We follow this, and we can flip this seat from Republican to Democrat for the first time since the late 1990s." Well, that was a bold statement. Chris didn't say anything, just smirked. He was, and is, a tough one to read so I wasn't sure if he was laughing with or at Bryan.

I opened the 20-plus page document past the table of contents to the first page that mattered—the summary page. This page provided the top data lines on the district's registered voter makeup, projected voter turnout, my "win number" (simply put, the number of votes I needed to win, and ultimately, the campaign's final goal) and maybe most terrifying of all (at least to me at that moment), the projected budget. All I saw glaring back at me was (what seemed to be) an unbelievable number.

$183,470

I sat there staring at that number for what must have been a little too long for comfort because after a while, Chris asked, "So, what do you think?"

"How. The HELL. Do I raise. $183,470?!" I shouted, repeating each section of that sentence very slowly for obvious effect.

"I told you he'd react that way," Chris said to Bryan.

"Look, it's really not that much," Bryan said as he tried to calm me down while simultaneously lighting a cigarette.

"How is it not that much?! You could buy a house for that!"

"When we get the wealthy LGBTQ community from South Tampa onboard – and they definitely remember Ronda's relationship with the community – I actually think this is the low end of what you'll be able to raise. And it's less than what the candidate raised in this district for the last election," Chris tried to cut in with his attempt at logic and precedent. *It wasn't working.*

I flipped to the section with the detailed finance plan, and as I suspected, I was already behind the planned fundraising pace by nearly $4,000. It was a fact that Chris and Bryan simply dismissed, saying I would likely make it up in the next month, even though we were about to head into the typical fundraising doldrums of early summer. They obviously had far too much faith in my thus far lackluster fundraising abilities.

The more I dug into the plan, the more dismayed I got. $5,000 for materials and campaign swag. $18,000 for polling and research. $24,600 for paid field personnel and door knockers. And the kicker—$110,000 for paid communication (mail and digital only with no current plan for radio and no money for TV), not to mention the other odds and ends that filled out the budget.

On the good side, my intrepid consultants pointed out that they expected the Florida Democratic Party and the County Party to kick in about $55,000 between them (similar to what they had done in the previous election cycle), so that alleviated my personal fundraising burden somewhat. Although they were telling me about all the help I should expect, my heart was still pounding just contemplating the numbers in the plan's budget.

"Look," Chris said, "we can absolutely adjust the plan based on fundraising numbers. We can cut down on paid staff and certain communications, or even wait until later after the primary to start, but at a bare minimum, we're going to need $150,000 to make this a competitive race."

"Scary money part aside, how will this differ depending on who wins the Republican primary?" I asked, trying to change the subject and internalize what would be required of my still-struggling fundraising abilities.

"We can cross that bridge when we get to it," Bryan said. "We don't need to start communicating about them until August, so we have time. Obviously, the messages will be different, but overall, the pool of people we want to communicate with is the same. We've already begun planning for that. Starting next month, we're going to be doing a series of "Adam positive" digital ads to start getting your name ID higher and prep people for more platform-based messaging later on."

"That's right," Chris chimed in. "For now, besides fundraising, we need you to start getting volunteers to knock on doors every weekend. The plan has that kicking off next Saturday. Since we don't have a primary, it gives us an advantage; we can start talking to non-party affiliated voters right now. The Republicans won't start that until after their primary is decided. We have a three-month window to work on turning those votes by ourselves. Let's make the most of that!"

"Great. How do we do that?" I asked.

"First, we need to design your palm cards. Flyers, basically. They're usually about 4" x 9" with some pictures and info about you and your platform. Something to hand out to potential voters at events and when knocking on their doors," Bryan explained. "I'll get you a couple old ones from past campaigns as examples. Chris, who do you have that can design those?"

"My team can definitely do that, and it's part of the budget. Design costs about $750 or so," Chris replied.

"What if I design them myself?" I asked.

"Candidates don't do that! If they do, the flyers always come out terrible," exclaimed Bryan, laughing at my suggestion.

"I do graphic design for my small business; let me give it a shot. I already did the stand-up banners and other swag. I think we're going to have to do everything we can to save money," I said.

"Okay, but if your design sucks, my team will take it over," Chris told me. My design did NOT suck, and we used it throughout the entire campaign. Take THAT, Chris!

"While you're doing that, I'll get us an account with NGP VAN through the state party; that will help us determine who we need to target when door knocking," Bryan added. VAN, the Voter Access Network, is an online product from the National Democratic Party that helps candidates target, plan, and track which voters they want to communicate with through phone, text or knocking on their door (canvassing). It's a bit cumbersome to learn how to use but is vital in maintaining a communications database. I would need it to "cut turf" by assigning which doors our volunteers would knock on.

"Who should we target once we have a VAN account?" I continued.

"At this point, any non-party affiliated voter who typically votes in a mid-term election, that has middle-of-the-road to slightly left-leaning beliefs," Chris said.

"Holy shit – VAN can tell me who those people are?"

"It sure can, that's why we NEED to get an account right now, and why we can get an advantage by identifying and talking to them early," Chris told me. "We persuade 3,000 of those voters to come to you instead of the Republican candidate, and we can win this election from just that."

"3,000?" I asked. "How do you figure that?"

"That's the difference between expected turnout and current voter behavior, and what you need to win. It gets you to your win number," Bryan said. "Basically, it's 50% of the expected turnout, plus one. We get you that many votes, and we'll be calling you 'Representative' in November."

Budgets, canvassing, VAN, win numbers ... I had a lot to digest in a short amount of time (as we used to say in the Navy, I was "drinking from the firehose" with so much new information coming my way). My next tasks were to design my flyers and palm cards and start gathering volunteers for weekend canvassing. The good news was that we had a plan down on paper. As I mentioned earlier, failing to plan is planning to fail, and I had no intention of losing an election because I didn't have a plan.

Adam's fundraising total: $15,327

Joe's fundraising total: $43,963

Ronda's fundraising total: $10,030

CHAPTER NINE

The Qualification Process

Adam's collateral set up at a candidate meet-and-greet the week of qualifying
Photo used with courtesy of the Hattersley Family

Chapter 9:
The Qualification Process

Most people think that once a candidate has filed to run for office, their name will automatically appear on the ballot. This, my friends, is not the whole truth. That initial filing simply lets the powers that be know a person's intention to begin a campaign and start raising money (which by the way, comes with its own reporting requirements from Day One).

The actual way to get a name on the ballot comes a little farther down the road through Candidate Qualification, a process that separates the real candidates from the casual political dabbler. Qualification involves a bit more paperwork, a personal financial disclosure, and proof of viability that comes in one of two forms, citizen petitions or a qualification fee. We'll talk about each.

The first item is the Candidate Oath and was also part of the initial filing process. It must be filled out once more, and serves to reaffirm your name, party affiliation, and eligibility to hold the office you are seeking. It must be notarized in Florida, and each state will have its own specific requirements described on their respective Secretary of State website (and also in the state-specific

Candidate Handbook, a handy guide to what is required in all aspects of a campaign).

The personal financial disclosure is a little more involved. This document lists the candidate's incomes, assets and debts, and shows your total net worth. It can get quite complicated, especially if you have interests in multiple businesses or several different sources of income. This form is used to show financial integrity and to make sure a candidate isn't personally bankrolled by a company or a political lobby. In a perfect world, no outside person or group would have undue influence on an elected official, right? Listing all sources of income can also be tricky, but many states accept the previous year's tax return for proof of this portion of the form. (Have you ever heard about a politician refusing to release their tax returns? This is the reason it's a touchy subject. Where do these people get all their money? Are they in anyone's pocket? Inquiring minds want to know.)

The last piece can either be simple or terribly difficult to process. The candidate handbook I mentioned earlier will describe the fee and/or petition requirements. The simple way is to make a payment to the Division of Elections from the campaign bank account; this payment is the fee option. It's (usually) prescribed as a certain percentage of the annual salary of the position the candidate is seeking. For my 2018 election, it was six percent. Done and done.

The hard way is through a citizen petition. To show local support, a candidate must submit a certain number of verified petitions filled out and signed by registered voters who live in the district you are trying to represent. Each district has a different number of required petitions based on the number of registered voters who live there (1% of registered voters for Florida), which for my district was just under 1,200 petitions. Additionally, the candidate must pay the Supervisor of Elections Office a fee (approximately 10 cents each) to verify each signature. Keep in mind that a campaign must reach the petition threshold with only people registered to vote in the district, so typically, a candidate submits a lot more than the number of required petitions just to make sure they get enough valid forms (and yes, there is a specific form, so printing fees for the campaign apply as well). Fortunately, the Supervisors of Elections accept petitions for a few months prior to qualifying, so a campaign can keep track of their verified, official progress.

How does one go about getting petitions signed? There are a few methods that should be used concurrently. Remember those club and caucus meetings I talked about? Those are great places to find people willing to sign a petition. A campaign can ask a local business if they can sit outside a heavily trafficked entrance and ask people as they come and go. And of course, the tried-and-true method—knock on a bunch of doors and ask people to sign. Party affiliation (or lack thereof) doesn't matter here, as long as the person is a registered voter in the district.

The qualification period is also usually only a business week long and for state offices (like the one I was running for) all the original hard copy paperwork had to be received in the Secretary of State's office in Tallahassee between noon on Monday and noon on Friday of the qualifying week. People running for county or local offices have the same requirement but only need to deliver their paperwork to the county Supervisor of Elections' office. Okay, now that we're all on the same page, on with the show.

Qualifying week was approaching, so being an organized former naval officer, I had all my forms filled out, notarized, and ready to go. I wrote a check from my campaign account, packaged up the bundle neatly, and sent it certified mail on the Friday before qualifying was officially open, so it was scheduled to arrive on Monday afternoon right after the qualifying period opened. Solid planning and execution, or so I thought.

I checked the state website constantly that Monday afternoon. Slowly, the names of candidates in all sorts of races from one Florida coast to the other began shifting to a "Qualified" status. Everyone must have had a similar plan to mine, and since the Secretary of State's office worked through the forms in order of their receipt, mine must have been farther down the stack than I anticipated. By the close of business that day, my name (and neither of my opponents' names) were listed as qualified. Not to worry, there was still plenty of time.

That evening I called Bryan.

"Hah-lllllooo?" his usual phone greeting drawled.

"Hey, it's me. I have a couple questions about qualifying," I said.

"You sent everything on Friday like we talked about, right?" he asked with a not so small amount of panic in his voice.

"Yes, of course!" I told him. "Not too many names have updated on the state's website, though. I just hope everything is okay."

"When they get to your packet, either the site will update with you being qualified or they'll give you a call to let you know what's wrong. Don't worry about it. Have either Joe or Ronda qualified yet?"

"Not yet – no one from my race has. What if I'm the only one to qualify?"

"If you're the only one? Well then, you win unopposed and there isn't even an election!" he said.

"Holy shit! Really?!" Suddenly, my hopes were up. "Does that happen often?"

"In a race like yours? No. At least one of the Republicans will qualify. Guaranteed. They hold the seat now and certainly won't give it up without a fight." *Wow, Bryan, thanks for dashing my hopes so quickly.*

"Oh, well, I guess I'll go back to checking the site every five minutes after the state office opens tomorrow," I said, maybe just a little let down.

"Don't do that! You need to be making fundraising calls! Focus on that!" he almost shouted at me. As I was starting to realize, this would be his default response most of the time anyway.

"You're right. I know you're right. I won't obsessively check the site," I (innocently) lied to him. What he didn't know wouldn't hurt him, right?

"Okay. Keep your head in the game. We're only about four months away from Election Day; things are only going to get more hectic from here on out. Make the best use of your time, that's the only resource a campaign has that it cannot replenish," he said and clicked off.

Not certain if that had been a pep talk or a scolding, I decided to at least try and put thoughts of qualifying out of my mind until the next day (Tuesday), when hopefully, that magic "Q" word would appear next to my name in the official record.

A meeting I had previously scheduled the next day was uneventful, unimportant, and sadly, unproductive. I was all the way across town though, so I decided to do some call time from a nearby coffee shop to let traffic die down before heading home. Headphones and the free Wi-Fi gave m *radio DJ* e a nice little bubble to plow through some phone numbers AND periodically watch the state website to see if I qualified to be on the ballot. Not a bad little setup, I thought.

The afternoon wore on and call time was ... well ... call time, which for me meant a frustratingly few conversations resulting in more people not wanting to bet on the predicted loser. On the bright side, I was at least crossing potential donors off my list that I didn't have to call in the future. The day was wearing on, and I was about to start packing up when someone called me for a change, and it was from a Tallahassee number.

"Good afternoon, this is Adam," I said as I answered the line.

"Mr. Hattersley? Good. This is the State Division of Elections. We received your qualifying paperwork, and there are a couple problems," she said.

Shit.

"There are two reasons why we cannot accept this for qualification," she began. "One—it looks like you personally signed the check for the qualifying fee, but a different person is listed as your campaign treasurer. Before you ask, it doesn't matter if you are listed on the account; the declared treasurer has to be the one to sign the check. Two—the notary stamp on your financial disclosure is slightly overlapping a line on the form and it obscures one number of the notary's license number, therefore, it is invalid."

You have got to be shitting me. This kind of crazy minutia can derail a political campaign? I was shocked, frustrated, and angry all at the same time.

"What do I need to do to fix it?" I asked.

"Well, you simply have to resubmit the defective forms. Get a check signed by your treasurer and a fully clear notarization of the disclosure and you should be fine. There's plenty of time," she told me.

After clicking off, my first call was to Bryan to describe our latest dilemma. His reaction was nearly identical to my own, but we made a plan to meet at our treasurer's office as soon as they opened in the morning, where we would get a new check. His office also had an in-house notary, so we planned on getting two versions of the disclosure stamped just in case we ran into another problem, we would have a backup. Once all the documents were in hand, the last step was overnighting the parcel directly to the Division of Elections office in Tallahassee. With luck, the new paperwork would arrive with about one day to spare in case there were any new problems we needed to address. Plan in place, I headed home to print out the items (including my prior year's tax return for the disclosure) for the next day.

Wednesday morning with the qualifying period already half over, I arrived at the small parking lot across the street from our treasurer's office about ten minutes before they opened. I paid for parking and only had to wait a short amount of time before Bryan pulled in. We went over our plan of the day, and he gave me a rundown of what we would have to do if this next batch of paperwork still wasn't "legible enough" for the state's taste.

"If you get another call with more problems," he started, "it won't be until tomorrow afternoon at the earliest. That will give us less than 24 hours to fix any issues and jump in the car to hightail it to Tallahassee in person. Clear your schedule for Friday just in case we have to leave early in the morning to get there before noon to hand deliver the papers." So far, my first experience with election bureaucracy was decidedly not going well. To put a second layer of urgency on our morning's mission, Bryan also decided not to pay for parking and roll the dice on getting his car towed. Great.

Once the office opened, it didn't take very long to get a new check. Bryan had called the previous evening, so our treasurer had one ready to go. The only pain point was waiting for the notary to get to work (she picked a fine day to be late). Less than 30 minutes after the office opened though, we headed out with the required documents in hand, and luck was, for once, on our side when we found Bryan's car still in its unpaid for spot. Hopefully, that was a good omen.

"Keep me posted if you hear anything from the state," Bryan told me, clutching the packet of my political future in his hands. "I'll try to same-day these to Tallahassee." Off he went to the post office, and I nervously drove back home to flail at fundraising all day.

Even though the papers were still, at best, in Bryan's hands in line waiting to be mailed, the first thing I did when I got home was check the state website. Of course, I wasn't qualified yet, but guess who was—one of my Republican opponents, Joe Wicker. He had run for office once before, so had more experience than I did when it came to election paperwork, and it shouldn't have been unexpected that he wouldn't have any issues qualifying. But it still gave me pause and made me think about this entire process.

What if I didn't qualify? I had raised my hand to run for this office when no one else would. I had made promises to give voice to those who didn't have one, and fight for those who couldn't fight for themselves. All of that might be dashed based on avoidable clerical errors? Not only would I be failing myself and my family, but more importantly, all the people who believed in me across the district—people who had already given their time and money to help me be successful. These were people who had been ignored and marginalized for decades and saw our little campaign as a way for them to finally be taken seriously by their own government. Going down this thought spiral did little to ease my nerves (nor did the extra-large latte I got on my way home that morning), and to say I was a little on edge would be a gross understatement. The thought of letting so many people down who were counting on me to make it on to the ballot at the very least was firmly rooted in the back of my head.

The rest of the day went by in a tangle of anxiety, which only ratcheted up when the uber-critical "qualified" notation showed up next to my other Republican opponent, Ronda Storms. Now, if I failed to qualify, the district would be guaranteed to stay in conservative hands. Hopefully, my nervousness wasn't too evident while I did my meager best to raise funds and waited to see if I needed to make an emergency trip to the Capitol.

Thursday morning dawned, and I still wasn't listed as qualified to appear on the ballot. With barely 24 hours remaining in the qualification period, most races had full rosters of candidates who were all apparently better at navigating the red tape than I was. Lunchtime came and went, and still no updates. Mid-afternoon snack? News free. By this time, I was resigning myself to a nine-hour round trip to Tallahassee to try and sort out any issues in person.

Right before I finished my call time phone list for the day, I decided to check the website one more time.

"Christie! It's up! I'm officially qualified!" I yelled when I saw what was (finally) on the official election website. Our paperwork saga of the day before did the trick—I was going to be on the November ballot! I let out a huge sigh of relief and sent Bryan a text to let him know we would not need to drive halfway across the state the next day.

There are a lot of takeaways from this. Diligence when it comes to dotting the i's and crossing the t's? Sure. Patience when faced with a period of uncertainty that cannot be moved along with more information? Absolutely. But maybe the biggest realization from this entire episode? Faith. Faith in our campaign's ability to adapt to a situation and overcome obstacles. Faith in our process. And maybe even a little faith in ourselves.

Adam's fundraising total: $18,809

Joe's fundraising total: $49,763

Ronda's fundraising total: $11,891

CHAPTER TEN

Independence Day Parade

Adam at the July 4th parade in his district
Photo used with courtesy of the Hattersley Family

Chapter 10:

Independence Day Parade

On the second Tuesday of every month the East Hillsborough Democratic Club met, usually at a small, local pub in the evening. This particular second Tuesday in June was no different, so Christie and I headed out to the meeting. This group was the Democratic backbone of House District 59. In fact, the group's president, Donna Lee Fore, ran for the seat herself in 2014, losing to the then-incumbent. The East Hillsborough Dems were always very supportive and willing to volunteer for local campaigns, so forming a close relationship was critical to my efforts to flip District 59 from red to blue.

The meeting that night was typical. They went over normal group business, let each candidate present speak for a minute or two, and then, during announcements, they discussed the upcoming Fourth of July parade. They always rented an old-fashioned trolly and wanted to know who from the club was going to march in the parade with them and who would be willing to arrive early to help decorate the trolly. And by the way, if any candidates wanted to march with them, we were more than welcome.

March in a parade? Get access and exposure to thousands of people from the district that I hadn't been able to reach yet? For free? I was in! And, as it turns out, the Brandon, Florida July 4th parade was, unbeknownst to me, the largest Independence Day parade in the Sunshine state. The parade had been run for decades, with a route starting less than three miles from my house, yet I had never even heard of it before. That should give you an indication of how little I was involved in the community prior to this political endeavor.

With a little under a month until Independence Day, we had some preparations to make. I designed and ordered a couple banners, t-shirts, and palm cards (glossy 4" x 9" two-sided flyers with my campaign info and platform) to distribute along the parade route. Between Christie and me, we were able to convince close to 25 friends and neighbors to march with us in campaign shirts and hype me up to everyone. Everything arrived at my house (AKA campaign headquarters) with plenty of time to spare before July 4th. So far, so good.

The day of the parade arrived, and while we had been told when and where to meet for pre-parade staging, the actual parade wasn't starting until 11 a.m., but with such a large event, the preparations took quite a while, so we needed to be at least 90 minutes early. With the Navy's "if you're not early, you're late" drilled into my psyche and my fear of parking problems, we arrived at the staging area just before 9 a.m. Not surprisingly, we were the first people from the East Hills Dems to arrive, and we sat there by ourselves feeling like idiots for nearly 20 minutes until someone else showed up. (This "sitting alone by myself because I'm early" motif will reoccur for me throughout the campaign, thank you, United States Navy).

While we waited, other groups that would be participating also began showing up. Local organizations, business and political candidates all gathered their troops. We even saw a truck drive by with a "Joe Wicker for State House 59" on it, one of the two Republicans running right here in my district. Whichever of the two won that primary would be my general election opponent. I heard the other Republican candidate, Ronda Storms, was also going to be in the parade, but at this point, I hadn't met either of them. They both had their own parade spots reserved and were up near the front with the other Republican candidates while I was at the back, with all the other less-funded groups.

As the morning wore on, more and more people filled up the giant parking lot serving as the staging area. Some were in trucks with advertisements, some came with bands, and some came with homemade floats pulled by an SUV or a pickup truck. And, as you would expect, lots of red, white, and blue everywhere. Suddenly, Christie and I heard our names being called out, and we looked over at a small group walking into the parking lot. A late 20s-ish woman was smiling and waving at us as she approached.

"Is that the girl we met at the NCAA meet in Ann Arbor?" Christie asked. Four years prior, my alma mater, the University of Michigan, hosted the Men's Gymnastics NCAA Championships, where I was one of the judges. The school had also hosted a reunion for those of us that had competed on the team throughout the school's history, and that was where we had met this girl. Her husband was on the Michigan Men's Gymnastics team a few years after I was, and they had attended the festivities as well.

"Oh my God, I think it is!" I replied. "That's Paul Woodward's wife, Julia! What kind of weird coincidence is this?"

Christie is usually great in social situations, no matter the circumstances. This time, though, was a little different. The only interaction Christie had with Paul and Julia was when the two of them were fighting, and that was what Christie remembered, so when Julia greeted her with a hug, all Christie could say was, "Great to see you! Are you even still married?"

Not the best way to greet someone after four years, but hey, it was a weird scenario.

"Of course, we are! I'm sure Paul says hello. So, what are you guys doing here?" Julia was either too surprised to respond as one would expect, or savvy enough to just move past the awkwardness of the situation.

"Adam is running for the State House! What are you doing here?"

"Oh, I'm Gwen Graham's campaign manager for her run for Governor. She's marching in the parade," explained Julia. "I'll make sure to introduce you to her."

Holy cow! Not only was one of the Democratic favorites for Governor marching in the same parade we were, but we happened to be (relatively) old friends with her campaign manager? Christie was right, this was a very weird coincidence!

"Gwen is scheduled to get here right before the parade starts, so we'll make sure to stop by your spot when she makes her way up to the head of the line," Julia told us. "Be on the lookout for us so we don't miss you!" she called over her shoulder as she went off to find her fellow campaign staffers. Marching in a big parade for free, and now we might get a photo opportunity with one of Florida's most prominent Democratic stars? Independence Day was turning into a red-letter day for our campaign, even greater than we could have hoped for!

According to the information we had, the time to line up for the parade start was fast approaching, so we headed to our assigned space while the trolly trundled its way through the masses. Our plan was to stay a little separate from the trolly to look like we were our own separate parade entry, and with a pretty big group all dressed the same in campaign shirts and sporting a few giant banners, we felt like we had a good shot of pulling it off.

We found our spot, and while members of the East Hillsborough Democratic Club were putting their finishing touches on the trolly, one of the people marching with us tapped me on the shoulder.

"Don't look now, but Ronda Storms is coming through the crowd in a golf cart," he said. I took "don't look now" as "wildly stare" and found myself literally right in front of Ronda. She looked at the signs and shirts around me, and with a giant smile on her face, grabbed my hand to shake it and introduced herself.

"I was wondering when I was ever going to meet you!" she said, beaming at everyone around us. "You have a great parade!"

"Happy Fourth of July," I said back, clearly surprised but trying to hide it. "Enjoy the parade, too!" And off she sped in her golf cart. What the hell just happened? I hoped that all our future interactions would be as simple and as (strangely) pleasant.

I was still fairly confused when guess who showed up next? None other than the as promised former Congresswoman Gwen Graham. The less-than-a-minute-long meeting was almost a carbon copy of Ronda's fly-by, but at least this time, I got a good photo. Wishing each other a Happy Fourth, she continued her way to the front of the parade. For better or for worse, the day was already strange, and just when I was gathering myself together again, the parade got underway.

We followed the trolly for about a quarter mile before we got to the actual starting line of the route. Being early July in Florida and close to midday, it was already swelteringly hot and humid, and most of the people marching with us had already sweated through their shirts. We needed a dedicated person to run fresh bottles of water to us from the trolly. Fortunately, the Democratic Club had the foresight to bring hundreds of bottles as this wasn't their first summertime parade. My little group of marchers were set up with campaign banners both leading and following our section, with the bulk of our force handing out my palm cards to as many people as we could who were watching the parade. I had brought close to 3,000 of the palm cards, so we had plenty to dole out. The hardest part was keeping pace with the parade when spectators would try to engage us in conversation along the route. Speaking of conversations ....

***

Comments from Christie:

Think about the last time you were outside on the hottest day of the year in the blazing sun and then amplify that by five, and that is what marching in a 4th of July Parade in Florida is like. You are hot, sweaty, dehydrated and there is a lot of waiting. I didn't realize this parade was such a big deal. In nine years of living in Riverview, I never realized there was a 4th of July parade right up the street – and one of the largest in Florida at that. This was, however, a good way to get some literature into the hands of people who would be voting in the next election and perhaps grow Adam's "brand awareness." Adam asked me to hand out our palm cards to the crowd, and I'm always happy talking to people. And if you just run up and hand someone something, they'll typically take it, even if they're not happy.

So, we started marching and as we're going along, a few of us "worked" the crowd. My standard spiel was something like "Happy 4th of July! Don't forget to vote!" after which I would stick a palm card in their hand. Most people were happy, and a lot would say things along the lines of "Thank you! I always do!" or "I'll take a look at his info!" Some asked questions like, "What does he do?" or "Has he run before?" or "Is he a veteran?" Some would say something like, "Tell me about him!" In some cases, I'd call Adam over to shake their hand. It was nice to actually talk to voters and hopefully make a positive first impression.

There are, however, always those that, no matter what kind of candidate you are, just don't care. Staunch Republicans or Democrats that, if you're from the other side of the aisle, who want nothing to do with you so they rudely hand the palm card back to you or say, "I would never vote for a Democrat." It's a sad state of our politics that we are so divided. Occasionally, someone would yell an expletive at you or give you the finger, but the people at this parade were generally polite.

Then, there are the people who literally aren't even on the side of the United States of America. As I was handing out literature and reminding people to vote, I came upon a few individuals sitting in lawn chairs watching the parade. In my chipper, overly enthusiastic way I said, "Happy 4th of July! Don't forget to vote!" and an older gentleman with a white moustache, a trucker hat and ripped flannel sleeves says to me, "I don't vote." He refused my literature and I said, "That's a shame, it's your right. Why don't you vote?"

In that moment, I knew that I shouldn't have asked the question, but I have very little patience for people who don't exercise their right to vote. The man looked at me and immediately replied, "My loyalty is to the Confederacy!"

I was stunned. I did not respond and went on my way. Did he realize he was at a 4th of July parade? Was he aware that the 4th of July celebrated Independence Day for the United States of America?! To this day, I am still not sure how to take that comment. I do, however, know that the memory of the Confederacy lives on in the hearts of many Floridians judging by the number of Confederate flags displayed in the parade. In some people's minds, the Confederacy should rise again and that is a truly scary thought.

In some ways, I'm glad this man did not vote but in others, I'm saddened that his hatred of this country was so blinding to him. I wondered if he ate barbecue and watched fireworks later that day, reveling in the celebration of a nation that he does not even support. It leaves a lot to ponder. One day, I hope he understands the irony of the whole thing.

***

Christie came over to me about halfway through the parade and relayed her run-in with the Confederate. I was floored! It was a hard moment of realization for me. I knew I was trying to represent people of all political leanings that lived in my district, but I really didn't understand the full range of those beliefs. Even there, watching the parade, there were people who were so far left they put Bernie Sanders to shame, all the way to my wife's new Confederate acquaintance. How can one person reconcile that extraordinary spectrum of viewpoints to represent them in government? Over 175,000 people live in our district, each one with their own take on how things should be done. Was I really up to the job I was going after? I quickly shook my head. I would have to deal with those thoughts another time, not when I was in the middle of thousands of parade-goers. Back to the task at hand.

About 45 minutes of marching the length of the two-mile parade route had us finally rounding the last corner. Along the home stretch there were crowds of people with squirt guns and fans – apparently a tradition at the end of this sauna-like journey. The folks lining the street were surprisingly polite and even made sure to ask before dousing the marchers, and I was more than happy to accept any offer of cooling water, no matter if it was shot at me or not. We even passed by a woman waving an "Adam Hattersley for State House" sign – it was my wife's manicurist, Betsy, right in front of her shop! It was a very pleasant sight as we crossed the finish line into a supermarket parking lot that served as the final rally point.

It was quite an experience, let me tell you. It opened my eyes to some stark realities that I had so far been sheltered from. Up to this point in the campaign, we had been courting Democratic support and volunteers, so we hadn't ventured very far into groups or organizations that were on the other side of the political spectrum. The parade was the first time really seeing voters that didn't agree with us and the experience made it more than clear that I needed to branch out and engage those on the conservative side as well. A candidate needs to talk to everyone. And be civil about it, too – as my brief meeting with Ronda shows, just because you may be political opponents doesn't mean you cannot be civil. Anger and hate divide people, making it a lot harder to win an election.

Also, don't be afraid to have some fun when you can. Ultimately, the parade was a blast. For most of the folks that came with us, it was their first time participating in a parade and everyone ended up with smiles on their faces.

One last thing: know your audience. Christie's run-in with the die-hard Confederate made me think of the ever popular "Florida Man," and how he was also a part of my district and targeted communication pool. "Florida Man" is a real thing no matter what state you are from, and every candidate may have to deal with him. News stories like "Florida Man Attacked During Selfie With Squirrel" or "Florida Man Who Tried to 'Run' to Bermuda in Inflatable Bubble Rescued by Coast Guard, Again" (both actual headlines) are simply indicative of a real part of our country's electorate. Other descriptive phrases like "Florida being Florida" or "Well, it is Florida" just accompany this motif—when you encounter something weird or unexplainable that you'll probably never understand ... that's definitely a "Florida" moment.

Adam's fundraising total: $20,554

Joe's fundraising total: $54,607

Ronda's fundraising total: $15,205

CHAPTER ELEVEN

A Candidate Forum

Candidates seated at the Bell Shoals Baptist Church forum
Photo used with courtesy of the Hattersley Family

Chapter 11:

A Candidate Forum

Candidate forums were another new thing for me. I had neither been to let alone heard of one before getting involved in this race. However, starting about four weeks before the primary election – late July or so – I was participating in up to four different forums each week. It was surprising that so many different organizations held these events, and how well attended they were considering how incognito they seemed to be amongst the general public. But, if you ever want to meet your local candidates and learn about their platforms, from the lowest office on the ballot (such as the Soil and Water Conservation Board) to those higher than you would expect (U.S. Congress and statewide cabinet positions), local forums are a great place to go. So, if you happen to drive by a large building within a few weeks of an election that has hundreds of different campaign signs planted all around it, chances are, there's a forum going on that night. And, yes, they are almost always held at night to get the largest turnout.

Hosting organizations run the political spectrum from left-leaning groups such as the University of South Florida's Student Government, to strictly conservative groups like the Plant City Chamber of Commerce. Unfortunately for me, living in a traditionally conservative area, most of the forums I attended were not the most welcoming places for Democrats. I knew that my race was going to be close, so (win or lose) nearly half of the district would not agree with my ideas, but having one-on-one face time with individual voters, most importantly, independent and moderate Republican voters, could make the difference. All I had to do was convince them to check my name on their November ballot. Easy, right?

The forum that this chapter focuses on was one of my first, held about a month before the August 28th primary election, at an extremely conservative mega church that sits smack dab in the middle of my district. This event was known across the county, and state, as a vitally important one to gain the considerably large Christian vote – and was also known as a staunch Republican stronghold. Every Democrat I spoke to, from this election cycle and past cycles, wanted to avoid the literal hate that they received by the event attendees. To give you an idea, I was one of only five Democrats to attend (out of more than 70 candidates). Not going to lie, I was nervous, and definitely NOT looking forward to it. But, if I was going to represent this area in the state legislature, I wanted people to know I was representing EVERYONE, not just the people on my side of the aisle.

Forums are held in numerous ways. Some encourage candidates to set up tables (like a trade show), some invite candidates to speak on a central stage, some encourage a panel discussion, and of course, some are a combo. This "Mega-Forum" was a combination of trade show tables and central stage speaking, but with tweaks to both formats.

Normally, for the trade show format, each candidate picks their spot based on a first-come, first-served basis. That way attendees got a good smattering of candidates and offices up for election and encouraged them to wander around to find those competing on the same ballot. It kept the forum's flow going and made for interesting and varied conversations. The version of the trade show that this Mega-Forum used, however, was a little different and almost … combative in my opinion.

Each respective office level had a small section of tables set up in a hollow square with candidates standing in the middle so people could walk around and approach all of them. That meant that in my square, I was standing right next to the two Republicans also vying for House District 59, and three other Republicans running in other House districts. (I was the only Democrat at this level to attend. Talk about enemy territory!) Fortunately, the two Republicans running in our district's primary hated each other even more than they hated me, so one of them walked the room instead of being forced to stand next to her primary opponent. Needless to say, tensions were high as I was ganged up on during the set-up phase by the four "hostile" campaigns that surrounded me. Luckily, my wife, Christie, was there to help. This event would have been a lot harder without her there.

An interesting side note: of the two Republicans running against each other for the chance (as all information indicated) to beat me in the general election, I had only met one up to this point at the July 4th parade. This was my night to meet the other one, Joe Wicker.

This wasn't Joe's first time running for this particular seat. He ran in 2012 but lost the Republican primary by a mere 175 votes in a hand recount. He had been waiting in the wings for the outgoing representative, Ross Spano, to leave the seat—either by term limits or by running for a different office. (After six years in the Florida House, Ross decided to run for U.S. Congress, so the seat was open). Ross had won re-election to this seat in 2016 by just over 9% (which is a lot actually), so Joe was licking his chops for another chance. All he had to do, or so he thought, was win the Republican primary and he was as good as elected to the Florida House of Representatives.

Like me, Joe was a veteran. He had served in the U.S. Army as an officer and done a tour in Iraq (sound familiar?). He had the backing of the Republican Party of Florida, who was dumping money into his campaign to ensure he was the nominee; in their view, it was "his turn" after all. Joe owned a small home healthcare company and had three kids. Picture your typical, white male Republican candidate. His unofficial platform consisted of three main points: 1) how much he loved Donald Trump, 2) how much he loved Donald Trump, and 3) how much he loved Donald Trump.

I introduced myself to Joe, who spent about two minutes to get to know me before he simply turned away to talk to another Republican candidate while I was in mid-sentence. Well, at least the semi-conversation went cordially. Christie questioned why I even bothered to introduce myself.

We finished setting up, and people started arriving; our political Trade Show was on! It took a while for attendees to filter back to where we were because the "higher" offices' candidates were closer to the main entrance. People waded through a statewide cabinet section, a U.S.

Congress section, and a State Senate section before they got to us, and we were before County Commissioners, the School Board, and various local candidates. It was smart that they held this event in the main lobby of the mega church, or else there would not have been room.

I had dozens of conversations with voters that night, but one in particular stood out. A sweet, grandmotherly Republican lady (she made that very clear right from the start) spent close to 20 minutes chatting with me. We discussed our families first, before going into political positions and ideas. We agreed on nearly everything: education, transportation, taxes, voting rights, business regulations, the environment – the bread and butter of any political platform. I was getting excited that I might earn her vote, mostly because I knew, by this point, that any Republican who voted for me was basically worth two votes (one for me, and minus one for the other guy). Toward the end of our conversation, I "went in for the kill" or as my sales-skilled wife would say, I went for "the close."

"I've really enjoyed talking with you, and hopefully I've earned your vote this November," I said, hoping for at least a knowing smile in return. What I received was something much different.

"You seem like a nice, smart young man but I could never vote for a baby killer," she deadpanned right to my face, loud enough for everyone nearby to hear before she coldly turned and literally hugged Joe Wicker, who was standing right next to me.

I was shocked. Christie was standing right next to me and was just as shocked (and furious). "What did she just say to you?" she said, not just asking, but actually questioning someone's audacity to say that to another person, let alone one standing in a church. This lady knew I was a Democrat; therefore, I must be Pro-Choice (which was true), and therefore, I was just so liberal that I wanted to kill babies. *What?!* That lone comment from that lone grandmother took me back eleven years, to the first time I had been called a baby killer.

Military Flashback

May 2007: I had been home from my year-long tour of duty in Iraq for three weeks. My parents flew up from Florida to visit me in Maryland (I was back teaching at the U.S. Naval Academy in Annapolis), and to meet my then-girlfriend, Christie. They had arranged for us to go into Washington, D.C. (only about an hour away from my house) to meet their congresswoman and have a tour of the U.S. Capitol. I drove all four of us to the New Carrolton metro station so we could take the subway into town, and since we were meeting a member of Congress, I wore my summer white uniform.

We were two stops from the Capitol as we pulled into the Potomac Avenue Station, when the woman behind us tapped me on the shoulder. I turned around and saw a woman in her mid-60s wearing hippie-era clothes. She calmly asked, "Why do you like to kill babies?"

"Excuse me? I don't! What?" I said, quite taken aback.

"Baby killer!" she screamed at me as she ran off the train, only to walk down the platform, get back on the train, two cars away, presumably to get as far away from me as she could. My parents, in the seat across from us, heard this exchange, and I could only imagine what was going through my father's head because he had been called a baby killer when he returned wounded from Vietnam in 1968.

The lady saw me wearing a uniform; therefore, I was a monster from her nightmares, and therefore, I killed babies.

Eleven years ago, an ultra-liberal called me a baby killer, and now an ultra-conservative was calling me a baby killer. I couldn't believe it. I felt just like I did in 2007, like someone had just punched me in the gut. A feeling that was really not great for one's confidence for the main part of the night, when we each had two minutes to speak in front of the nearly 2,000 people in attendance.

"Don't listen to her," Christie whispered so only I could hear it; she had seen the Republican candidates nearby smirking at the woman's comment. "The organizers are calling for all the candidates to go backstage. Get your head on straight and go get 'em!"

She was right; I needed to focus on the next, and arguably most important part of the evening. It was each candidate's chance to make an impression on the entire crowd, and not just the individuals who we spoke with earlier. All of the candidates filed into the "green room" (a backstage holding room that the pastors used to prepare themselves before going onstage, and very similar to what you see in theaters. This church was gigantic, and their Sunday service was more of a show). There was quite a spread of snacks and refreshments waiting for us, and most of the Republicans chatted in little cliques.

I had the chance to meet a few more candidates (all Republicans, who always seemed put upon whenever I approached – how dare I say hello to them?!) while we waited. Once all 70 or so candidates were assembled, the head pastor gave us the rundown of how this portion of the event would proceed.

"First off, I am the moderator. I will introduce each race and the candidates vying for that office, starting with highest on the ballot and going down from there. Sit in your assigned seat on the risers on stage until your race is called, and then file down to the row behind the lectern designated for the speakers. All candidates will remain on stage in the risers until your race is called, and once everyone for your race has spoken, file off stage back to the green room. Each candidate has two minutes – which I will strictly enforce! – to make your speech. Any questions?" He was very concise. "No questions? Good. Line up in the order we give you and be ready to go."

Being prior military, I listened to the instructions and took my place as assigned. Being politicians though, everyone else ignored the head pastor and continued their conversations. Two assistant pastors went around to each little group to send the candidates to their places, a process which took another 10 minutes. Meanwhile, I stood in line by myself looking like a complete idiot. It "seemed" like another bad omen for me, which of course, did little help to my confidence.

Finally, the group was ready, and we started filing out. We were arranged alphabetically within each race, so for my race, I was first, followed by Ronda Storms and Joe Wicker behind me. Before we got to the stage, Ronda tapped me on the shoulder and asked to go in front of me (as I said before, she and Joe appeared to hate each other) so she would not have to bear her perceived travesty of sitting next to Joe for the approximate hour before it would be our turn to speak. Sure, why not, Ronda – after all, I'm here to help.

Walking out on this stage was pretty surreal. The theater (simply the best way to describe it) had nearly 3,500 seats, and a lighting and sound system that would do an off-Broadway production proud. The crowning jewel was a 25-foot light-up crucifix centered over the stage. There was a giant two-minute timer (at the back) that would stare at us to remind us of our time limit. The auditorium was about two-thirds full, so I would guess that just over 2,000 people were in the audience and most of them belonged to this church.

The production values were high, and the show started with the presentation of the colors, the National Anthem, and a prayer; it almost felt like we were at a baseball game. The head pastor then "threw out the first pitch" by explaining the same rules to the crowd that he had given us backstage. With that out of the way, he called up the first set of the evening's speakers.

While the first few people were speaking, I was able to look around more. There were giant screens set to the sides of the stage, projecting whoever was speaking in giant high definition. And with my luck, there I was, just over the right shoulder of the person at the lectern. Seeing myself big as life on these screens, I realized that I could barely move without sticking out like a sore thumb to the entire audience, giant crucifix over my head and all! And believe me, with all the super-conservative, Trump-loving rhetoric spilling out of the Republican speakers, it was extremely difficult not to wince. Fortunately, I found Christie in the crowd, and opted to live vicariously through her winces and surprised reactions.

The candidates filed through, and after about an hour of hearing Republican after Republican talk about the same three themes of guns, God and greed, we got to my race. Finally! The head pastor called for "House District 59 candidates to come to the front," and the three of us headed down. Joe sat in the first chair, I sat next to him, but Ronda made a point to stare daggers at Joe, and then move (I'm not kidding) 12 seats away to the far side of the stage. Joe and I just looked at each other a bit confused, as the pastor looked at the three of us equally confused.

As I was up first alphabetically, the pastor introduced me (and of course, butchered my last name) while I walked up to the lectern. Knowing that this crowd was hostile and that I only had two minutes, I planned to alter my typical stump speech. I simply couldn't talk about LGBTQ equality, women's rights or climate change in this environment and expect to leave with my head still on my shoulders, so instead, I pulled the tried-and-true, pure and All-American card – I talked about my time in the military, with some uncontroversial issues sprinkled in.

"Good evening, my name is Adam Hattersley, and I'm running for the State House right here in District 59. I'm a veteran and a small business owner. I spent eight years in the United States Navy as a nuclear submarine officer, and I served a tour with an Army unit in Iraq from 2006-2007. One thing I've noticed, everybody up here has been talking about their September 11th stories, and I have a September 11th story too, so please bear with me. I was doing what's call OHARP, the Officer Home Area Recruiting Program, in Ann Arbor right after commissioning and before going through the Nuclear Power training program.

We thought we were going to have a line out the door on September 12th. And I know that a couple of candidates have mentioned that they joined up right after, and I definitely applaud them for that. But where I was, nobody showed up, and we were really surprised. We went in town and asked people why and they said, "It's not my problem, they'll do something about it." We can't wait for "them" to do something about it, it's up to us. We have to stand up and make changes.

One of those changes that I really want to talk about is education. Here in Florida, we're in the bottom 20% in the country in education funding, and we pay our teachers dead last in the country. Any teachers in here? A few? I've been endorsed by the Hillsborough Classroom Teachers Association, and this is one of my priorities. We need to give our kids and our teachers the tools they need to excel.

Now, I don't have all the answers, and I wouldn't believe anybody who says they do have all the answers. But what I do have is a moral compass. It's that same moral compass that led me to join the Navy and volunteer for the submarine force. The same moral compass that led me to volunteer to go to Iraq so that another sailor could stay home. And it's that same moral compass that I think will represent you, the people of the 59th, in Tallahassee.

I appreciate you listening to me, thanks for coming out tonight, and I'll appreciate your vote in November."

I think it was the right message for the audience. I was feeling pretty good even though my nerves were still on edge as I went back to my seat. After all, I had no idea what the two Republican candidates were going to say. Would they stay on message like I did, or would they attack me, or each other? Turns out, they were out for blood – just not mine.

It felt to me like they were tearing each other apart, berating their primary election opponent every which way—from not being able to do math, to equating the other to a strange lighthouse—a joke that no one seemed to understand. It was hard not to smile up there on stage while the two of them demonstrated each other's real and made-up faults. Between the two of them, they talked about close to zero policies or platforms, instead, they mostly focused on how terrible the other one was.

When they finished, the three of us filed off stage, with Ronda and Joe keeping as much distance from each other as possible. Feeling like I had done as much good (or as little damage) as I could have, I met up with Christie and we dismantled our trade show booth as quickly as possible while the stage portion was still going on for several races below mine on the ballot. This event had been quite the emotional roller-coaster.

I learned a lot from that forum beyond trying to let toxic comments from strangers roll off your back and how to speak to the audience you're given. Maybe the most important takeaway was that no matter how hostile, no matter how opposed to your ideas, a candidate cannot be afraid to walk into any room if you plan on representing the people in that room.

Adam's fundraising total: $24,574

Joe's fundraising total: $62,857

Ronda's fundraising total: $17,731

CHAPTER TWELVE

Friends and Frenemies

Patton campaigning for his dad
Photo used with courtesy of the Hattersley Family

Chapter 12:

Friends and Frenemies

As the August primary election neared and we were war-gaming strategy for both Republicans in the race – good to be prepared – I was put in touch with a veteran Tampa Bay political operative named Bret Evenson. Bret had been on the scene for quite a while and was known for being the "man behind the man" for several successful elected officials. My consultant, Bryan, had asked Bret to discuss his thoughts on my prospects for the general election on November 6th.

This was a big deal for me. Getting a chance to meet a real politico like Bret and get his advice promised to be a huge learning opportunity for me. What was I doing right? What was I doing wrong? Where did I need to focus my efforts? If I impressed Bret enough, would he entreat his connections on my behalf? A lot was riding on the meeting, and Bryan reminded me (several times) under no circumstance to start the conversation without him. He felt the need to protect me. Sweet of him, no?

The day of the meeting came, and honestly, I was a bit nervous. I had gotten comfortable with my small group of candidate friends and their spouses, but Bret would be the first "operative" that had ever actually won a legislative race that I would have the chance to talk to. Bryan was worried for two reasons: 1) Bret might try to steal me away, or more likely 2) Bret would crush my poor little candidate soul.

We had agreed to meet at a small restaurant equidistant between Bret's office and my house, and per usual, I arrived 15 minutes before our lunch meeting. Since Bryan was my only example, I figured all political operatives worked on their own timetable, so I was caught off guard when Bret arrived two minutes after I did. Great. Now there was no way to avoid Bryan's precondition of not starting without him. Nothing to do but dive right in at this point.

Bret and I found a table and settled in to get to know each other. I was hoping Bryan wouldn't be his normal 15-minute-late self, because if he was, I would be on my own with Bret for close to 30 minutes – the exact scenario we (or was it just he?) wanted to avoid. I tried to stall a bit and drew out the small-talk portion of lunch, but as there's only so much time to waste in the political world, before long, we started discussing the meat and potatoes of my district and my campaign. Bret cut me off after about three minutes.

"I took a hard look at the 59th this morning before coming over here, and I'm going to give it to you straight," he said. "It's a Republican-drawn district on the Republican side of the interstate where no Democrat has won since God knows when. The Florida GOP is already pumping money into it to keep it that way, too."

"That's news to me. The Republican candidate hasn't even been decided yet; why would the state party already be playing?" I asked.

"A couple reasons. First, they want to make sure the seat stays red, so they're doing some general conservative messaging. Second, they've already decided to back Joe Wicker; he's their guy and the district's heir apparent. The Republicans want him in Tallahassee, so he's their safest bet to win."

"Do you think the state Democratic party will jump in and help me?"

"No way in hell. They made a huge investment in the district last cycle and got creamed. I checked where the money is going, and the 59th isn't one of their targets this election," he told me. "House Democrats are going to struggle to even keep the seats they have now and don't have the cash to branch out to pick-up districts. Honestly, if they did, they still wouldn't dip their toes in the water here. It's a loser."

"Okay, so what do you think I should do?"

"Keep running your race and follow your plan – that's really all you can do. Oh, and pray that Ronda wins the primary," he said.

"I already am. Bryan and I think she'll be easier to beat than Joe."

"She might be *possible* to beat. If she wins the primary, the race will be close, but you may have a slim shot. If Joe wins ... you lose by 15 points." He dropped that hammer in such a nonchalant way I almost missed it. Now I understood why Bryan didn't want me to meet with Bret alone.

Do keep in mind, though, that Bret is good guy, and he wasn't saying these things to be malicious. He was simply being honest. The best people in politics are the ones who will give you the information or analysis straight. Decisions that affect wide swaths of people are made in this business, and those decisions are better served with the truth, regardless of feelings. I didn't like what Bret was saying, but I absolutely appreciated his impartial take on the race. Even though we had just met, he respected what I was trying to do enough to not sugarcoat what he saw as the reality of my district. Knowing that logically in my head was one thing, but that didn't stop Bret's words from crushing my poor little candidate soul.

About 30 seconds after Bret dropped the bomb that my entire campaign effort was essentially a waste of time, Bryan finally joined us.

"What did I miss?" he asked, sliding into the seat across from me.

"Just about all of it," Bret told him as he started to get up. "And now I have to run. Great meeting you, Adam. Best of luck and let me know how I can be helpful."

I waited until Bret had left the restaurant, then gave Bryan a full download of the conversation. His jaw nearly hit the floor.

"That's why I wanted you to wait until I got here!" he said. "I've always known Bret to be direct, but holy shit! He sure didn't pull any punches."

"He just told me how he saw it," I said dejectedly. "Maybe he's right and I should just quit and save everyone the time and effort."

"Don't you dare think that way! We've gone over the data with a fine-toothed comb. You know the district is winnable. Chris knows the district is winnable. I know the district is winnable. Take Bret's input as just another data point but trust the plan. You can do this!" Bryan was in full pep-talk mode.

Was he right? Of course, he was. Was I still going to sulk during the car ride home? You better believe it.

I knew it was going to be hard getting over the debacle of a meeting I had just sat through, but I had to trust in my team, trust in my data, and perhaps most of all, trust in my purpose.

The big discovery moment that solidified my resolve came later that day when I recounted the meeting's details to Christie. The more I talked, the more I realized just how much I cared and how much I wanted to win. She simply looked at me and said, "So, go win."

I'll be damned if I'm going to let her down.

Frenemy Help

A few days after getting my ass handed to me by a fellow Democrat, I was back in the forum circuit. This time, it was the Riverview Chamber of Commerce hosting candidates from all over the Tampa Bay area. If I was ever going to have a "home-field advantage" for a forum, this was it. Riverview is my hometown, and the venue was less than half a mile from my house.

My wife and I had convinced several of our neighbors to attend the event, so I had a small cheering section lined up. And we would need every last one of them since the Chamber was also conducting a straw poll during the event. A straw poll is basically a mini-election held among event attendees, and can be a huge confidence boost (or confidence crusher) for the candidates. This being a conservative-leaning Chamber of Commerce event, I didn't think I had a chance to win the straw poll, but our neighbors would at least make it look like I had outperformed expectations. I'll take any version of a win I can.

Like all the other candidates and their teams, we set up a table with information and campaign swag, ready to greet the event's attendees. There were people running for everything from the local school board and county commission, to statewide and federal offices. Big campaigns and small ones, the forum drew candidates from several surrounding districts as well, so the place was packed.

The first part of this forum was easy—stand by your table and talk to voters face to face. The second part was going to be something new for me though; each candidate would get a turn at the lectern to be asked a few questions by event moderators. This would give the audience a chance to see each race's candidates one after the other to help convince them who they would not only cast their ballot for in the evening's straw poll, but in the actual general election in November. Gulp.

Once again, realizing the event was sponsored by a Chamber of Commerce, my heart fell a little bit at the prospect of being asked leading questions by conservative moderators who would try to put their thumbs on the scale a bit, and not in my favor. I grabbed an event program to find out who the moderators were, and my mood took a quick turn for the better. Yes, one of the moderators was a well-known, local super conservative, but the other was a good friend of ours who was on the liberal side of the spectrum. The event organizers went for fair and balanced for a change, and I knew that my fellow Democrats and I would not be alone on the hot seat during the question-and-answer portion of the forum.

I shared this bit of information with Christie, but instead of showing what should have been optimism, I had a pained look on my face.

"Are you feeling okay? You look a little ... green," she said.

"Is it hot in here? I'm not feeling great," I replied.

"No, it's freezing. Why are you sweating so much?"

I looked around the room and sure enough, everyone had a couple extra layers on and looked uncomfortably cold. But by this point, I was taking my suit jacket off and my stomach was doing flips.

"Um, I'm feeling a bit nauseous," I told her. "Why do I keep tasting Chinese food?"

"You didn't eat the leftovers for lunch, did you? I meant to get rid of them!" She seemed a little panicked.

I loosened my tie and unbuttoned the top button of my shirt, trying to cool off. I was in for a struggle with my own guts, and the timing couldn't have been worse. The question-and-answer part of the night was supposed to start in 10 minutes, and every candidate needed to take their places soon.

"I'm going to pop outside and try to cool down. I'll be right back," I whispered to Christie, nearly running out the door.

I paced back and forth just outside the venue trying to lower my rising temperature (I worried that I would have to make a mad dash to the bathroom), and after a few minutes, I heard that announcement, "All candidates to your places!"

Shit.

I walked back inside and went straight to my seat near the stage. I was the only candidate without a suit jacket and looked like a sweaty hipster before a failed job interview. Definitely not at my best. We were all set up by ballot, so I plunked right down next to one of my Republican opponents, Joe Wicker.

"You feeling okay?" he asked me after shaking hands.

"Sure! Just feeling a little nervous," I tried to cover. We had about 45 minutes of other candidates to get through before it was our turn. He was keeping a sidelong watch on me in case he had to jump away from any vomitus accidents.

Honestly, I can hardly remember the event from then on, I was so focused on keeping my composure (and my lunch). I absentmindedly watched as each candidate received their grilling, unable to determine who performed well and who flopped. My turn came and went, and I think I answered a question about healthcare? Strange coincidence since in the back of my mind I was thinking about seeking healthcare at that very moment.

After another half hour of misery in the candidate section, the formal part of the event was done. I made my way back to my table where Christie was waiting for me.

"You did great! You looked relaxed and sounded confident!" she said, welcoming me back with a hug. "Are you feeling any better?"

"I just want to hear the results of the straw poll and get out of here," I said, looking around. People had been filling out their ballots race by race as the speakers took their turns, so most were already putting them in the collection box. The event organizers had promised results within about 15 minutes of the final speaker.

We started closing up shop at our table, hoping to time the results with the conclusion of our packing so we could bolt for the door (and maybe the restroom again). The event's emcee said he would announce the straw poll winners very shortly, and to stick around to hear the news. A volunteer made a show of handing him the list of ballot totals, and every candidate held their breath in anticipation.

"The votes are in! Starting from the top: the winner for U.S. Senate is ... the Republican!" he started. "The winner for Florida's Governor is ... the Republican!" Every race was called the same way. No surprises at all.

U.S. Congress Districts 14, 15, and 16: Republican

State Senate Districts 19, 20 and 21: Republican

State House District 57 and 58: Republican

My race was next, and naturally by this time, I thought it was a foregone conclusion.

"The winner for State House District 59 is: Democrat Adam Hattersley!?" the emcee announced with a questioning voice. What the hell?

My wife and neighbors went nuts! Every single straw poll winner that night was the Republican, *except for my race*. Talk about the home-field advantage!

Or so I thought. We finished packing up, and Christie was already at the car. I headed for the door carrying our last box of supplies, but heard an unfamiliar voice call my name before I got there.

"Hi, Adam. I'm the campaign manager for one of the Republicans running for office, and just wanted to let you know that I think you did a great job tonight. Honestly, I'm not a fan of your opponents, so I asked my team, and our supporters, to vote for you. Good luck!" he said smiling before turning to walk away.

Suddenly it made sense why I was the only Democrat to win that night—unknown to me someone had stacked the odds in my favor. It was still nice to win, but it made the night's excitement seem somewhat hollow. The only buoying thought was maybe the Republicans this gentleman spoke to on my behalf would remember that when the actual Election Day came around.

Was I disappointed I hadn't *really* won the poll? Some. Was I still happy with the reaction from the crowd and at least "the appearance" of local support for my candidacy? You bet.

Thinking about the past week provided me a lot of lessons to digest. A candidate for political office may have some surprising detractors from within, *but* a candidate may also have some unexpected support from normally hostile places. Ultimately, I decided that I simply could not count *anyone* out.

Adam's fundraising total: $27,256

Joe's fundraising total: $67,507

Ronda's fundraising total: $17,831

CHAPTER THIRTEEN

Campaign Staffing

Amy Bolick, Adam, and Cassidy Whitaker
Photo used with courtesy of the Hattersley Family

Chapter 13:
Campaign Staffing

Campaign staff are the unsung heroes of American politics. You always hear about the campaign manager as having the "big job," but there are so many roles on a campaign that are not only critical but may rival the campaign manager in importance. These roles can also greatly vary from full-time paid staffer to casual volunteer. So far, my campaign had (at best) some casual volunteers – we could barely afford the trickle of digital ads we had running, let alone a person. This cash-flow conundrum didn't stop Bryan calling to talk about staffing up though.

Before we dive into that, here's a quick primer on the top two or three campaign staff roles. These are by no means the only staff a campaign could have, but simply some of the most vital (and keep in mind that every campaign is different, so staffing decisions really do reside with the candidate, so be flexible). And as always, fundraising will determine who, and how many staffers any campaign can hire. That being said, here we go:

Finance Director – for larger campaigns, the Finance Director is the first hire any forward-thinking candidate should make. Fundraising really does dictate what your campaign can do, how it communicates, and who else it can hire. The Finance Director title itself tells you most of what you need to know about the role: this person creates the plan and directs the strategy to get your campaign more money. They help plan and execute events, design digital fundraising efforts, and most importantly, plan the candidate's call time. They find phone numbers, conduct research on potential donors, and follow up on pledges. Frequently (on smaller campaigns), they even sit in a room with the candidate while they are making phone calls, which is its own role in large campaigns. For even bigger campaigns, this person directs the whole finance team, which may have multiple positions all designed to fund your greater efforts. Any finance hire should raise you more money than they cost you or else, why hire them?

Campaign Manager – the campaign's "Jack-of-all-trades" so to speak. They work with the candidate on strategy, coordinate the other campaign staffers and any vendors the team is working with (campaign swag, digital vendors, ad buys, strategy and polling, mail pieces, etc.). This is the candidate's "right hand person" (or, for you military types, the Executive Officer to the candidate's Commanding Officer) and they will usually attend all events with the candidate. In all honesty, this person is also responsible for "managing" the candidate themselves, because after all, candidates can get in their own heads sometimes.

Field Director – this person directs the campaign's "field" effort with door knocking, phone calls and text banking. They will determine what geographic areas to focus on, and using special software, assign individual doors (or phones) for volunteers to contact. They will work with the Campaign Manager to figure out what demographic of people are the best to contact, then carry out that face-to-face plan. If you've ever gotten someone at your door wanting to talk about a political race, they are carrying out the Field Director's plan.

These roles are different from the **General Consultant** (if you have one), in that the GC can be working for multiple campaigns, and the above staffers are on *your* campaign only. Okay, now that we're all on the same page, on with our story.

Bryan called me about staffing the campaign up a little. He knew we couldn't afford a full-time anything (and in fact, knowing our cash struggles, he had waived his own fee more often than not on his own initiative. He *really* had his heart in this campaign and wasn't working on it for the money). But he thought we might be able to hire a part-time field staffer to help get my name out in the district more and cover the crucial door-knocking program. He wondered if I could think of anyone who could fit the bill.

I told him about a recent college graduate named Cassidy that had reached out to Christie, and who lived in our district. She was currently working as a paid field person for an old friend of hers, who was already a state representative and now running for re-election to a second term. Cassidy was interested in us for several reasons. She wanted to help a campaign in her own district, her current job required a long commute, and she was working 10-hour days in the hot Florida sun, knocking on over 100 doors every day. All that aside, her biggest reason for wanting to help us was that the campaign she was currently on was for a deep-red Republican, and

Cassidy was a Democrat. All good reasons, wouldn't you say? I thought so.

Bryan agreed that a conversation with Cassidy was well worth our time, so we arranged to meet her at a local coffee shop, which, I must admit, often acted as our unofficial campaign office because of their free Wi-Fi. So, early one morning before the normal workday began, Christie, Bryan and I were all sipping our lattes when Cassidy arrived, exactly on time. Good first impression, something Christie and I both mentioned while she was inside getting her cappuccino. Bryan simply lit another cigarette with a slightly grumpy look on his face; he knew who Cassidy was currently working for and was skeptical of her motives for contacting our campaign.

Cassidy joined us with her coffee and a smile on her face; she seemed truly excited to have a chance to work with us. Bryan went right in on her.

"Why the hell are you working for the campaign you're on right now?" He sounded almost like a prosecuting attorney.

Cassidy looked a little taken aback, "Um, well, I've always wanted to work in politics, and I went to high school with my boss, and I didn't know any other way to get a start. My boss is my age, and a woman – and I think that's important. Besides, I'm only a paid canvasser; I don't have a strategic role nor do I even have much contact with the candidate. I want a *real* job in politics, not just knocking on 100 doors each day."

"Don't you *know* who your candidate is working with? Have you ever talked to him? *DID HE SEND YOU HERE?*" Bryan wasn't letting up an inch.

What neither Christie nor I knew, was that what was really bothering Bryan was the campaign that Cassidy was coming from. Not that she was working for a Republican, but that *this* particular Republican shared a General Consultant with one of the other candidates running for the same seat that I was running for. A General Consultant that was known to hold no punches, and Bryan (unfoundedly, as it turned out) suspected him of sending Cassidy to spy on us. This was a level of paranoia that we really didn't expect, and since Bryan wasn't sharing his concerns with us, both Christie and I were surprised by how he treated Cassidy at the start of our meeting.

"Hold on a minute," I said. "Cassidy, relax. Tell us a little about yourself." While I was trying to get poor Cassidy's attention away from Bryan and give her a chance to gather herself, my wife was staring daggers into my consultant's soul.

"Um, I went to St. Leo University and just graduated this Spring," she said, still obviously flustered. "I've always wanted to be involved in politics and campaigns, and I've lived right here in this district my entire life. Christie, you met my mother, right?"

"I have! She is lovely, and your dog is adorable!" Christie was doing her very best to make Cassidy feel comfortable and welcome.

***

Comments from Christie:

I am a salesperson, so I use all modes to talk and meet with people including phone, email, Whatsapp, LinkedIn, etc. I believe that if you're not using all channels available to you, you're limiting yourself. During the campaign, I found Facebook messenger was a great way to reach out to new people and chat. Sometimes, people would message me out of the blue with questions for Adam or advice. I once decided to message some folks that were commenting on the former Representative's page and ended up finding out we had a friend in common, a person that I went to high school with. We connected and realized that not only did we live around the corner from each other, we were politically likeminded! It was a new couple for Adam and I to grab a beer with in our area.

In another one of these instances, a girl named Cassidy Whitaker sent me a message. She explained that she was a student who just graduated from St. Leo University and wanted an "Adam Hattersley for State House" yard sign. She said that she was working, but that I could drop it off at her house because her mother was home. She gave me her address and in between calls for work, I traveled just down the road to her house with two signs in tow. It wasn't very far, but I'm still not familiar with all the neighborhoods out here. She said she was at the end of her street and could put at least one, if not two signs up.

I didn't know what her house looked like, so I followed my app's directions to the end of a street. There was a fence and behind the fence was a large driveway leading up to a small house that had tons of vegetation around it. At least that is how it looked to me. The sign in the yard said "Beware of Dog" and honestly, the thought went through my mind that perhaps this wasn't such a good idea, and maybe I shouldn't be delivering signs on my own. I walked up to the house and knocked on the door, but no one answered. I decided to leave the signs by the front door and get out of there as quickly as possible. As I started back toward my car, I heard a dog bark behind me. I got to my door and felt something scratching at my leg.

It was a little corgi, and now there was a man on the porch of the house who said, "Hey, are you with the campaign?" I responded "Yes!" and he said, "Come on in!" I was still a little scared though, but judging by the friendliness of the corgi, I wasn't as intimidated as I was when I first arrived. I walked inside and met a woman who was seated on the couch with a very friendly face. The man walked away but she said, "Hi, I'm Carol. I'm Cassidy's mom!" She was so warm and lovely to me. I said "Hi, I'm Christie Hattersley. Adam's wife. I'm just dropping off signs."

She told me to have a seat and continued, "I'm so happy Adam is running. I talked to Alex, and he said he canvassed with you on the Hillary Campaign, and he said you and Adam are such good people." I vaguely remembered Alex but thought it was so wonderful that someone actually remembered me because of the absolutely minor role I played in that campaign. I was just a field person.

She also said she knew Cassidy was interested in campaign positions because she was working for a Republican. She told me all about Cassidy's accomplishments at St. Leo and her interest in the political world. I was impressed, and honestly, in politics, the negativity can get so overwhelming that when you meet likeminded people who are welcoming and friendly, it's like a breath of fresh air. We chatted a bit longer, and she told me about her sales background, her travels, and that she was so proud of everything her daughter was doing. I stayed at their house chatting for 30 minutes or so before I gave her my cell number and told her to have Cassidy call me. I didn't know if we had a position open or if we could really afford one, but since it's always good to meet new people and network, it never hurts to chat. I said I would follow up on messenger, too (multiple points of contact!). Carol gave me a warm goodbye and I went back to my car with a smile on my face and an *excitement that people actually knew who we were. In my head, we were still nobodies.*

✻✻✻

"So, why the hell do you want to be on this campaign? *This* campaign in particular," Bryan interjected. He was convinced that this poor, innocent girl was meeting with us under false pretenses. And both Christie and I could tell that his aggressive attitude and questions were starting to get to her.

"What do you mean?" she finally asked. "I want to work for a Democrat, and even more so, one who has a chance to be *my* representative. I want to help put someone in office who I actually agree with, instead of people that have been there my entire life that hate everything I believe in!" She was definitely on the defensive now.

"And you're telling me that *no one* sent you here?" Bryan was relentless, and Cassidy was starting to tear up.

"Okay, that's enough!" Christie was about as close to snarling as I'd ever heard her. "Bryan, you are going to play nice, or you are just going."

Bryan seemed (strangely) a little surprised, but I could see the relief on Cassidy's face. We chatted for another 20 minutes before everyone headed home, and I was in for an earful when Christie and I got back to ours.

"What the hell was that!? What was Bryan thinking!?" Christie yelled at me as we were walking in our front door. "How can he think it's okay to treat someone like that? That poor girl! I really think you should consider firing him!" *She was steamed!*

"He's the only one who knows what's going on in Tampa politics, and I can't fire him," I said. "Don't worry, I'll talk to him about how he treated Cassidy. There aren't many people who believe in us like Bryan does; I can smooth it over and keep him happy."

"I think you should hire Cassidy. Give her a chance to show Bryan what she's made of. THAT would make ME happy."

"I can't make you both happy," I said. I was losing ground quickly.

"I'm your wife! You're *supposed* to make *me* happy!"

"We don't have the money to hire anyone, regardless. I don't think I can make *anyone* happy." Luckily, that broke the tension, and Christie's face cracked a smile.

"Yeah," she said. "I guess that's true. But I'm still mad at Bryan. You'll talk to him, right?"

With the situation on the home front restored to a normal level, next on my list of things to do was call Bryan and let him know how he treated Cassidy wasn't appropriate. Apparently, middle-aged LGBTQ men didn't really have a lot of experience talking to 22-year-old women.

About a week later, we had a photographer at my house taking professional campaign headshots. Of course, Bryan was there supervising us. He was in my back yard smoking a cigarette, standing next to Christie, the two of them watching while I was trying my best to remember everything from the one season of a reality tv modeling show I had once seen. Suddenly, Christie burst out laughing, and when I looked at them, they were both smiling and sharing a chuckle.

Turns out, Bryan realized that Christie was right and that he hadn't treated Cassidy very well, and the more he thought about it, the more he wanted to give her a shot. Before coming to our house that morning, he called her to offer her a job on his other campaign (a County Commission race) in a much better role than her current position. He felt we needed, at the very least, to get her working for the Blue Team. Welcome to the family, Cassidy. You're home now.

Finding the right staff is important. Sometimes the most qualified on paper isn't necessarily the right person, though. Look for the people that mesh with you and your team; you're going to be spending a lot of time together, so personalities have to be considered. If a staffer believes in what they're working toward and believe in the candidate, usually they can grow into whatever the campaign needs them to be. A lot can and should be said about the power of people working toward a common cause. *People Power.*

Adam's fundraising total: $29,493

Joe's fundraising total: $80,027

Ronda's fundraising total: $18,331

CHAPTER FOURTEEN

The Primary

Martin McClelland and Nick McMurdy
Photo used with courtesy of the Hattersley Family

Chapter 14:

The Primary

Fast forward a couple weeks. It was Primary Election Day, August 28, 2018. Since I didn't have a primary challenger, it was a (relatively) normal day for me. Campaign and fundraising calls, stressing out about the little (to no) attention we were getting no matter what we tried – typical super-underdog type stuff. I was, however, extremely interested in the outcome of the day's balloting; not only because it would determine who would be both parties' nominees for Governor and U.S. Congress, but by the time the clock ticked over to midnight, I should know who my general election opponent would be. Plus, depending on who that opponent was, I would know if I had any real chance of winning or not. It was a big day for my little campaign, and I had absolutely zero control over its outcome.

One of the people who got me into the whole election mess was in his own three-way primary for U.S. Congress in our district – Andrew Learned. Local support seemed to be firmly in his corner, and I was planning on attending his election night watch party that evening. A prominent businessman (and campaign contributor to both Andrew and I) was hosting the event at his office, luckily only about half a mile from my house. I would be on my own that night since Christie was in Boston attending a conference, so I would be without my 'secret weapon' and my campaign's best networker. That was fine though – it was Andrew's party, after all.

The Florida polls close at 7 p.m., so the watch party was scheduled to start right about then. The good thing about Florida's election laws (Surprise—There's some good in there!) is that Supervisors of Elections are allowed to count, but not publish, both mail-in and early voting ballots as they come in, so a significant part of the results are available minutes after the polls close. Although they are not complete results, they give a good idea of who will win early in the evening, especially in a primary.

Why especially in a Primary and not as much in a General, you ask? Florida's primaries are "closed." That means that only Democrats can vote in the Democratic primary, only Republicans can vote in the Republican primary, and people not in either party simply can't participate (unless there are candidates from only one party on the ballot, which means the race is open to all voters). So, since each primary has a voting pool that is more or less similar, one can assume that the results both before, and on, Election Day will be similar – regardless of when people voted. For some reason, in a General Election, Republicans tend to vote on Election Day rather than vote early, which means that early returns tend to skew Democratic, with Republican votes gaining ground as the ballots come in. If a campaign in a General Election is savvy, they will know how much ground to expect to gain (or lose) based on those trends, so early results can still be a solid indicator of overall performance before all the ballots are officially in. *Phew!* A lot to absorb, right?

Once again, I fell victim to my Navy training and showed up at 7:00 p.m. – right at the start of the party – and once again, I was the first person there. Not even the party's host, or Andrew, or any of his staff had arrived yet. Great. You would think I would have learned by this point, but promptness was just too ingrained in my DNA. Knowing I would be alone for a little while, I took a quick walk (and burned off some nervous energy) hoping that more people would have arrived by the time I returned.

The walk gave me time to think about my own campaign, and its direction over the next 10 weeks until General Election Day. Florida's primaries are *super* late, so with only 10 weeks between the Primary and General Election, it makes for a crazy sprint to the finish line compared to the relatively gentle pace of the campaign so far. The short time frame posed several problems but also featured some silver linings.

Good news: I would be able to call my campaign donors back to ask for more contributions. Florida law limited pre-primary giving for State House and State Senate candidates to $1,000 per person but provides a "reset" after the Primary. That meant I was basically starting with a clear playing field and could ask the (few) people who had already given that magical $1,000 for a second check.

Bad news: Republican fundraising in Florida typically spikes after the Primary, especially for the winner of a contested primary since that person could now call his opponent's supporters, too, so I could look forward to being even more vastly outraised and outspent.

Good news: We were now only 10 weeks away from the end of the campaign, no matter what. The long, slow slog of the past few months would seem like a fun stroll through the park compared to the upcoming schedule, but it would now (finally) feel like we were moving toward our end goal.

Bad news: We were now only 10 weeks away from the end, and the pace those weeks promised would be brutal. Did I mean to say brutal? Yes, yes, I did.

Good news: I would know who my opponent was. We were hoping that Ronda Storms would win the Republican primary that night, and in the following weeks, we could really use that to tap into the overly patient and wealthy LGBTQ political giving circles, who had been waiting for the Primary results before opening their wallets. They were very ready to bombard my campaign with all-important resources if it meant beating Ronda.

Bad news: Polls for the Republicans were trending toward the "safer" choice for their party, Joe Wicker. According to some major local political insiders in the Tampa Bay area, if Joe won the Primary, he would almost assuredly defeat me in the General. If Joe won, the entire race for District 59 would be relegated to a media footnote as a foregone conclusion.

Very bad news, indeed. Not to mention that instead of the two Republicans spending time and money beating each other up to win tonight's Primary, the winner would now spend time and money beating ME up – something we had thus far avoided.

That's where my head was as I meandered around before the party, and even though she was in Boston, Christie must have figured I would be experiencing a mental death spiral that evening, because before I returned to the party, she called to see how I was feeling. I can always count on her to keep me focused and looking for positives. She reminded me that we had plans for either scenario of how the Republican primary played out, so I should stay calm and optimistic. Before she rushed back to her conference, she told me to "Walk into every room like you own it – you belong there – be confident!"

Thanks, honey, I needed that.

I took a deep breath before walking back, and by now the party's host was there. It was a good opportunity to catch up with him, and gently let him know that my campaign would be open for ALL donors in the morning. He is a savvy guy, and he got the hint; score one for the good guys. Slowly, more people arrived and were focused not just on the food, but on the giant-sized news telecast on the wall, courtesy of a theatre-grade projector. We all watched the slow crawl of election results as they scrolled across the bottom of the screen, superimposed over the news channel's political reporter giving his analysis of early returns. There were a lot of contested primaries in the heavily populated Tampa Bay area, so the crawl took quite a long time to cycle through every race and update.

Andrew arrived around 7:30 p.m. to a group of about 30 people, right when some of the races were starting to show early results. His race covered three counties, so the final returns would take a while to come in, but he was optimistic and joking with his supporters in attendance. The newscaster was focusing on the gubernatorial races for both parties, seeing as they were both hotly contested – two-way for the Republicans (Trump's anointed vs. a Central Florida golden boy), and five-way for the

Democrats (everyone thought it would be a showdown between two of them, though – moderate vs. far-left progressive).

The room's mood was jovial, but a bit tense. Many of Andrew's supporters were on the more progressive side, so the crowd had a favorite for the Democratic gubernatorial nominee. I was rooting for the moderate candidate, but had to remind myself that most people who volunteered for campaigns, especially at this still relatively early date, tended to be on the farther fringes of their party's beliefs. The TV reporter was talking to a graphic showing statewide results as being too close to call yet while emphasizing that viewers should stay tuned in for updates. He did, however, have an early call for the U.S. Congressional race in District 15 (Andrew's race), and a new graphic appeared on screen. Andrew came in second, a distant second – he lost.

Bad.

The margin was over 21 points in favor of the candidate from the center of the district, Kristen Carlson. It was just after 8 p.m. and the room's mood took a major nosedive. Someone said that Andrew was outside calling Kristen to congratulate her, and he would come back in a few minutes to speak to the group. His staff, volunteers, and supporters had thought they would be gearing up for a nationally watched congressional race, but instead, their 18-month campaign journey was coming to an unanticipated and harsh sudden stop. Andrew and I had already discussed helping each other in the General Election, and now I would have to struggle to retain his volunteers' enthusiasm alone and try to convince them to work on a lower-profile race – while at the same time, court Kristen and convince her to join forces. The night was already providing challenges, and it wasn't over yet.

While everyone else was disappointedly chatting, I was watching the slow crawl of election information at the bottom of the screen. The news I got next was not any better than Andrew's — Joe Wicker won his primary by over 10 points.

Shit.

My heart sank. I figured that no matter what happened over the next 10 weeks until the General Election, I was now destined to lose. Prediction after prediction from the state's top politicos lent near certain credibility to that end — if Joe Wicker was the Republican nominee in my race, he would be the next Representative for District 59. He had the party machine, the money, and apparently, the local support needed to easily sweep into the seat. If I wasn't in my head before, I certainly was now, looking at the enormous mountain in front of me. I don't even remember hearing what Andrew had to say about his race. I was focused on my future as a solo mountain climber as I sat by myself in a corner of the room mulling over my options. As I mentioned, Andrew had been running for nearly 18 months, so his announcement was a huge blow to his fans. I sent Christie a simple text message before leaving: "I just lost."

Echoing what she had told me on the phone earlier that evening, she simply texted back: "Be confident. You. Belong. There."

She was right.

Sometimes in politics, you're going to have a bad day. Or get some bad news. Or lose. But, as I was learning

(or maybe Christie was trying to teach me), a politician
... even an accidental one ... has to do more than take
things in stride. They must project confidence. They
must persevere. Even in the face of long odds or defeat,
they must keep up the will to fight. You simply cannot
fix problems in the law unless you win.

Adam's fundraising total: $29,718

Joe's fundraising total: $82,077

Ronda's fundraising total: $19,831 − Eliminated from the race

CHAPTER FIFTEEN

The Pros and Cons of Canvassing

Daniel Pemberton and Adam canvassing in the district
Photo used with courtesy of the Hattersley Family

Chapter 15:

The Pros and Cons of Canvasing

Has anyone ever knocked on your door to talk to you about a political candidate or issue? They will typically wear a shirt about their cause, have flyers to distribute, and carry a clipboard. If so, you have been canvassed. Canvassing is a campaign's way to meet the people it is trying to persuade, a technique that has been proven to be an effective way to garner swing votes. It is also difficult, frustrating, and time-consuming work. It is both the bane and the savior of any political candidate.

My campaign had begun weekend canvassing in early June and had been doing it consistently since then. Each week, we would request volunteers using social media to reach them and would sometimes coordinate with other campaigns that overlapped our territory to maximize our reach. We had piggybacked with Vanessa Lester, who was heavily involved in the local party and had the responsibility for overseeing canvassing in our part of the county. Every Saturday, the group would meet at our local coffee shop to get their assignments. Since I didn't have a primary opponent, we were able to focus on non-party affiliated voters (Independents, also known as NPAs) for persuasion from the very beginning. We knew we would win or lose based on the share of votes that went our way from this group.

I had 47 voting precincts in my district, and we had a plan for canvassers to hit them all. We even had a couple of "Super" volunteers (a volunteer that supervised others and really went above and beyond), like Rebecca Myers, who told us that they would handle their home precinct for us. All we had to do was get them campaign materials and they would be off to the races. Love and cherish your super volunteers; they are few and far between and very much needed.

Notwithstanding the few precincts that were already covered, we still had tens of thousands of doors to knock on. My district held over 110,000 registered voters, and we were expecting a higher-than-normal mid-term turnout of over 60%. That's a lot of ground to cover, so we had to be strategic. Just another reason why people like Vanessa and Rebecca are so critical to electoral success. A good June Saturday had Vanessa planning our volunteers to knock on over 1,200 doors – that's a lot of potential votes that early in an election season!

A New Player Has Entered the Game

Now that the state had determined its Democratic gubernatorial nominee, most smaller campaigns were taking direction from him and participating in the "Coordinated Campaign" when it came to canvassing. This effort distributed lists for door knockers to use for voter persuasion, which was based on the needs of the Governor's race. We used these lists one weekend and found that we were only talking to deep-blue Democrats – people who always voted our way and were eager to vote. Basically, our Democratic base. Every campaign needs these types of voters, but since we can usually count on them coming out to the polls no matter what, engaging them this late is the game is redundant, and not the best use of limited resources. As we got farther into the summer, though, we had to take a bigger role in planning our *precise* canvassing needs that met our *precise* goals.

Enter Amy Bolick. Amy was in her late 20's and was heavily involved with our county's LGBTQ caucus and served as their political director. She worked at the University of South Florida and has two Masters degrees, but her real passion was politics. She and I had talked a few times at different events about how she could be more involved in my campaign on a professional ("paid") basis, however, I never had the financial resources to make that a reality, even though her help was badly needed. Fortunately, Amy wouldn't let something as simple as money stand in her way when she called me with an idea.

"Hello, this is Adam," I said, answering my phone.

"Hi, it's Amy from the LGBTQ Caucus. I was hoping to talk more about joining your campaign in a more official manner – I think I have an idea," she said.

"You know, we would love to have you on board," I told her. She is not only brilliant, but an extremely hard worker, the kind of person any campaign would be lucky to have. "What's on your mind?"

"Well, you know I have to work since my wife is still in nursing school, but I still have plenty of time in the evenings and weekends. I want to help with the field program, canvassing, texting and phone calls. I can take all that over to really target the people *your* campaign needs to target. I've already started digging into the data from the past three election cycles and know exactly where we should knock on doors, for the next four weeks at least."

Was it just me, or did it look like we were getting a Field Director for free? I was praying that it wasn't too good to be true!

"Wow – that sounds amazing! I'd love to take a look at what you've already done."

"Great! Are you still planning on canvassing this weekend? If you give me access to your VAN account, I can start planning where your volunteers should go right now," Amy said.

"No problem, I'll text you the info. Amy, I can't thank you enough for this, and I'll see you on Saturday," I replied.

"I'll see you there. Oh, and I'm going to bring a couple people from the LGBTQ Caucus to help out, too. The whole group really likes you, and some of them want to get more involved in the district. Heck, instead of watching TV in the evenings, I can even start texting potential voters, too. Really get things moving!" she told me before hanging up.

I felt like I just hit the jackpot. Finally, the campaign was going to be more than just Bryan, my wife, and I. We were threatening to look like a real, organized campaign!

The Good, the Bad, and the Funny

Regardless of the planning or the number of doors knocked on, canvassing means a lot of new human interactions. And, in Florida, a lot of new human interactions means plenty of opportunities for strange things to happen.

Sure, we would run into people that simply warmed your heart. They cared about their community, were excited to talk about it, and they really wanted to reach the ears of those vying for public office. There were people who supported what we were trying to accomplish, and even people who would gladly display one of our yard signs and/or speak to their friends and neighbors on our behalf.

We would also knock-on doors of people who would rather see us tarred and feathered than lower themselves to talking to a political campaign. We got yelled at, doors were slammed in our faces, and sometimes, we were even threatened. Most of the time, however, no one answered their door, and we would simply leave our literature in a little plastic bag on their doorknob. A good canvassing day had us face-to-face with about one person out of every six doors we knocked on.

Out of the thousands of doors I personally knocked on, there is one that stands out above the rest when it comes to a good canvassing story. Christie and I went out together (we liked to send our canvassers in pairs; even though it was less efficient, it was safer), and we were close to the end of our list for the day when we knocked on a door to a corner house in a typical suburban neighborhood.

As per our normal operating procedure, we waited a minute after ringing the doorbell before trying again. Another minute passed, and we were about to go to the next house when we heard the door unlock from the inside. *Score!*

As the door began to open, I checked my notes to make sure to ask for the correct person – in this case, a 32-year-old man registered to vote as an independent, but with slightly liberal-leaning tendencies. The exact bread-and-butter kind of voter we were looking for. The person who opened the door though, was completely unexpected. A four-year-old (at best) little girl wearing a swimsuit, shorts, sandals, and oversized purple sunglasses smiled up at us.

"Hi!" she cheerfully grinned up at us.

I was confused. Christie was confused. Since when did (let's be honest) babies greet strangers at the door? We looked at each other before Christie replied to the toddler holding the door open. "Hi! Is your daddy home?" she asked.

"Daddy doesn't live here ever since Mommy said she doesn't love him anymore," she innocently said, still smiling.

I didn't have a response to that.

Christie didn't have a response to that.

Luckily, we were saved by the aforementioned mommy.

"Hey! I told you never to answer the door!" We heard someone yell from the back of the house about five seconds before a woman in her late 20s came bounding up to grab her daughter.

"They're looking for daddy!" the little girl exclaimed.

"I kicked that bastard out last month. What do you want with him?" The woman asked us.

I wasn't touching that with a 10-foot pole.

Christie wasn't touching that with a 10-foot pole.

Instead, we went the neutral route.

"We're just checking in on the neighborhood's registered voters. I'm running to represent you in the Florida House of Representatives. Do you have a few minutes to chat?" I asked.

"That depends," she said, looking at us a little sideways. "Are you a Democrat or a Republican?"

"I'm a Democrat," I said. This question is always, obviously, a make-or-break moment with most voters.

"Oh, thank God!" she said, relieved. "I've just been so sick of everything I've been seeing on TV. We need a change. I'll put a couple signs in my yard for you if you have any."

Now, that was a surprise! I ran to the car to get some signs (candidates should always be prepared) while Christie told the lady a little bit about our campaign. We had her vote, and by the time I was back with the signs, Christie had her commitment to convince her friends to vote for me, too. This visit had started as one of the strangest moments we had canvassing but turned into quite a boon and definitely a high return on investment.

Political Chicanery

Nearly, if not all, campaigns do some form of canvassing. So, it should come as no surprise that my General Election opponent would also conduct door-knocking activities. He had targeting tools and volunteers, flyers, yard signs and t-shirts just like we did. My campaign couldn't afford to pay anyone to canvass for us, so we relied on volunteers, but Joe's camp certainly could afford them and he had them going out every day. Even though history, money, and polling all favored him, he was still putting in the work on the ground like any serious candidate should. I had absolutely no problem with that, especially as I was confident that if we both knocked on the same door and spoke to the same person, my message would usually be received better.

That said, I knew there were some extremely strong Republican neighborhoods that honestly, just wouldn't be worth my time to visit. Conversely, my district had some extremely strong Democratic areas that I really felt were my turf, and wanted my opponent, Joe Wicker, to steer clear of. Keeping that in mind and trying to take advantage of all the easy opportunities, I had convinced close to 20 of the households in my neighborhood to not only vote for me, but to show their support with one of our yard signs. My neighborhood was absolutely, and visibly, my turf.

I was on the phone in my home office trying to dredge up campaign contributions in the middle of a work week in September when I received a short text from my wife.

<Are you okay?>

That seemed out of the blue. Very confused, I wrote back.

<Yes. Why? What's up?>

<I've been getting dozens of messages from our neighbors asking if we're okay. They keep saying someone is after you?> she replied. Now I was really confused. <I'm freaking out! Why didn't you pick up when I called?> I hadn't even heard my phone ring, but sure enough, I had three missed calls from Christie.

I looked out our front window, and there was a strange car parked in front of my house with a man leaning on the driver's side door, that had "Joe Wicker for State

Representative" placards on it. Now I understood why my neighbors were so worried; my political opponent was staking out my home.

"Oh, hell no," I said aloud, even though I was alone.

I ran upstairs to put on an "Adam Hattersley for State House" t-shirt, then headed outside for a chat. This was *my* neighborhood.

"Hey! Can I help you?" I called out.

The man leaning on the car glanced up at the sound of my voice, and then his eyes grew about as large as they could when he recognized me.

"Joe?" He shouted, looking at my next-door neighbor's door.

Lo and behold, Joe came striding down my neighbor's driveway less than six feet from *my* yard. His buddy pointed at me, and when Joe saw what he was pointing at, his face got the look of a kid caught stealing from the cookie jar.

"Hi, Adam," he said. "I didn't know you lived here."

I guess I would have to take him at his word on that one.

"Yeah, and as you can probably tell by all the signs, I've had plenty of time to talk to my neighbors about the election. You guys okay? It's pretty hot out here, need some bottled water?" I tried to get a little snark in there and still stay polite.

"Very kind of you to offer, but we have to head out," Joe said as he opened the passenger-side door of his campaign car. "See you at the next forum."

Off they went, from what may have been the most awkward political encounter for both of us the entire election cycle.

As I walked back into my house, I had a nice chuckle about the whole situation, and for the first time, felt like someone other than Christie or Bryan had my back. It turned out that no less than eight different neighbors had called to warn my wife that there may be some shenanigans going on.

There are a lot of different tools at a candidate's disposal. Sometimes a scalpel is needed for precision, sometimes a hammer for force. But when a campaign is really looking for high return on investment, canvassing can be the precise hammer to bang home the message in the most effective way possible. Face-to-face or what's known as "retail" politics can be an absolute game changer in an election. Run your own game, just know that your opponent is running their own, as well.

Bottom line: the ground game wins races. Make full use of it.

Adam's fundraising total: $30,434

Joe's fundraising total: $84,577

CHAPTER SIXTEEN

The Importance of Star Power

Kerry Kriseman, Mayor Rick Kriseman, Mayor Pete Buttigieg, Christie, and Adam
Photo by Kim DeFalco

Chapter 16:

The Importance of Star Power

As I've said before, the political structure in the U.S. is much flatter than you think. Chances are, you're connected to political leaders at various levels, but you just don't know it. In my case, my wife had (at the time) more of those connections than I did. For starters, she used to work with the daughter of the Speaker Pro Tempore of the New Jersey House of Representatives (unbeknownst to us at the time). Random, I know but these connections can go a long way in smaller campaigns. Enter, Bryan ...

"We need some star power, someone to do an event for us and really draw a crowd. Do you know any celebrities?" he asked both Christie and I over speaker phone one day.

"I don't ... Christie?" I asked.

"I did an internship in college with the "Shadow" Senator for D.C. but I haven't spoken to him in almost 20 years. I think he's friends with some important people. I'll call him." Christie comes through, again!

Senator Paul Strauss, besides being a major advocate for D.C. statehood, was indeed friends with some important people. And even better, he clearly remembered all his interns ("we're family!" he called them). He not only donated to my campaign on the spot but said he would float the idea of coming to Tampa for an event with some of his more well-known, politically active friends. This idea was starting to look good.

A couple days later, Senator Straus called us back – he may have a bite! A very well-known actor (from one of my favorite TV shows, no less), said he would be amenable to flying to Tampa for a fundraiser. Only a couple of stipulations though:

1. A first-class airline ticket from one of either of two West coast cities (he was shooting a program and didn't know where he would be)

2. Two extra days in Florida (staying in a resort he was "accustomed to") for post-event golfing, to which I was not invited.

Looking into these requirements put the cost of his trip alone close to $20,000 – a sum we could hardly afford and would in no way recoup with the event. We had to scrap the idea of famous actor #1 coming to Tampa. Don't worry, he wasn't very broken up about it.

Our next idea also revolved around my wife's contact list. Christie went to high school (Go Dumont Huskies!) with someone who would turn out to have a big impact on my political career. Jennifer Holdsworth had started in local New Jersey politics right out of college. Volunteering on campaigns, canvassing, getting into finance, and managing campaigns. Then, she moved onto a more national stage with bigger campaigns: congressional, senatorial, and gubernatorial until she started her own political consulting firm in Washington, D.C. She became the regular left-leaning voice on major national news and political shows like *The Hill*, and on Fox News. Jen was big league.

So, we gave her a call. She and Christie caught up for a few minutes, then Christie told her about our campaign.

"I know this call seems pretty random, but my husband is running for the Florida House."

"I saw that on Facebook! That's great! I'm guessing you called to talk strategy," Jen replied, nailing it.

We told her about our district, who I was running against and perhaps most importantly, our fundraising struggles.

"How have events been going?" Jen asked, hitting the nail on the head again – after all, this was why we had called.

"A few small house parties, nothing big. All the same people show up to everything; it's been hard finding a new audience."

Quick aside — A house party is pretty much what it sounds like. Someone (a friend, relative, or supporter) offers to host the candidate at their home and invites neighbors and friends to meet you, listen to your stump speech, ask questions, and hopefully, contribute to the campaign. These smaller (and hopefully, frequent) events are a big part of retail politics and help get the candidate in front of more people, more often. More formal fundraisers are a little different, hopefully bigger, and not necessarily inside your own district, with fundraising being the main goal.

"We were hoping you could think of someone we could bring down for a bigger event and use it to encourage new and wealthier people to engage with the campaign."

"Hmmm ... let me think about who would be good, I may already have someone in mind," she replied. At this point, I had no idea who Jen was thinking of but I knew she had contacts all over the country. My only trepidation was the cost to the campaign like in attempt #1.

"Let me make a few calls, and I'll get back to you," she said.

We didn't know this, but in the year prior, Jen helped a friend of hers by running his campaign for Chair of the Democratic National Committee. They knew going in he didn't have a great chance, seeing as he was only the mayor of a mid-sized Midwestern town, but they thought it would be a good opportunity to start raising his profile on the national stage. The town he was the mayor of — South Bend, Indiana. His difficult to pronounce name was Pete Buttigieg. Luckily, everyone knew him simply as Mayor Pete (and if you don't know who Mayor Pete is, I'm not really sure why you're reading this book).

Anyway, a few days later, Jen called us back.

"Have you guys heard of Pete Buttigieg?" she asked.

"No," Christie and I said in near unison.

"Well, he's the mayor of South Bend, Indiana, openly LGBT ... which is a first in the Midwest and he is seen as a rising star in the Democratic Party. I've known him for a few years, and I ran his campaign last year for chairman of the DNC. He's super smart, a Navy veteran just like Adam, and he's interested in getting his name out all over the country."

A gay mayor from the Midwest? This could go a long way with the "money gays" (Bryan's term, who, by the way, was fangirling HUGE at this point) of South Tampa that we were struggling to engage with. Okay ... what do we have to do?

Jen gave Bryan's contact information to Mayor Pete's scheduler. Jen had already smoothed the way with Pete, and he was interested in coming down. Now we just had to work out the details ... date, venue, food, photographer, contacting guests, and getting contributions, in other words, the whole special event planning thing. This event was going to be the largest and most important undertaking that we would have tried so far in our campaign. We knew that we were going to have to pony up a bit of money on the front end just to get him down here. Flights, hotel, deposit for the venue space, and food. Pete was planning on traveling with an aide, who would set up meetings for him in Orlando the day after the event. The proverbial "kill two birds with one stone" trip.

Knowing all this, once we added up our estimates, we realized it was going to cost well over $2,000 just to put this thing on. Crap. Bryan got his task list and was off to the races. My job was getting people to not only come to the event but contribute to the campaign for the privilege. Again... *crap*.

Bryan and I kept each other updated on planning and progress. He found a great venue that we had recently been to for a state senate candidate's fundraiser, a nice, South Tampa French restaurant called Mise en Place. Bryan knew the owner, she was flexible on the date and the best part was that she was a Democrat and said she would "in kind" the venue fee, but we were on the hook for food and drinks. Now, when it comes to booking events, getting any type of in-kind offer is absolutely amazing since it means free. Several things can be done in kind, and perhaps the best thing about something being given for free is that the "donor" issues the campaign a receipt that you can claim as a campaign contribution. Which it is, just in goods or services rather than cash. So, in kind (which is subject to the same donation limits as traditional monetary contributions) means not just saving money but also adding to your fundraising total. Doesn't get much better than that!

We were off to the races. The venue was set, and we agreed to pay for some appetizers and have a cash bar. We had plenty of campaign signage to decorate the venue with as well. No one could look in any direction without seeing a Hattersley for State House sign or banner. The room was set up perfectly for events like ours, with plenty of tables and even a small, raised dais for speaking.

Bryan's progress: Location, food, drinks... all set

Adam's progress: No people committed to coming (yet)

Bryan was still working with Mayor Pete's scheduler on a date, but we were closing in on the first two weeks of September. That gave me a little more to work with when talking to people about the event. I had started announcing a possible event with Pete about mid-August, so there was already a bit of buzz, but ironing out a specific date was crucial. Bryan called me to relay some good news.

"We have a date! Friday, September 7th – Pete and his aide will fly down that day and get here just in time for the event," he said.

"That's great! Have you heard of any other events going on that night? It would be great if we were the only game in town," I replied.

"I haven't heard of anything yet, but I'll keep my ears open. We need to book two hotel rooms for the night of the 7th. I'm thinking that chain hotel in Ybor City. Since you have the campaign debit card, can you handle that?" Bryan asked me.

"Not a problem."

As soon as Bryan and I were off the phone, I called the hotel to book two rooms. They told me I would have to prepay for the rooms in person, since I was using a debit card. Looks like I had a trip downtown for the next day. Checking on planning:

Bryan's progress: Location, food, drinks, date... all set

Adam's progress: I have to drive to Ybor City tomorrow? Still no one committed to attending.

Booking the hotel was simple even though we found out two days before the event that Pete was coming alone, so I had to take yet another drive into town just to cancel the second room. Finding attendees now became the focus.

How does one wrangle up people for an event like this? Some word of mouth, some online and email advertising, but to really nail down RSVPs... the 'ole reliable — call time. Luckily, I had a little help. While I was dialing all the big political donors in the Tampa Bay area, the county LGBTQ Caucus (good friends and great supporters of our campaign), who were very excited for Pete's visit, pushed the invite out to their members. The top two DNC members in Central Florida (who lived in Tampa) were also on board; they had met Pete when he was running for DNC Chairman and were understandably impressed. Pete's staff also reached out to the Mayor of St. Petersburg,

Rick Kriseman, who he knew from the National Mayors' Convention. The guest list was shaping up.

The week before the event, the county's Democratic Executive Committee (DEC) – basically the county party – held their monthly meeting. They always recognized candidates and gave people the opportunity to make salient announcements near the conclusion of the night. It was the perfect time to make a last-minute pitch to get people excited to attend our event. *I'm so there.*

The meeting went like most of their meetings (sorry, DEC!) ... boring and slow. But, as they were wrapping up, the chair asked for any announcements. I made my way to the front and was ready to pounce.

"Good evening, everyone! I'm Adam Hattersley, running for State House District 59. We are having a fundraiser this Friday, the 7th, at Mise en Place at 5:30 p.m. We have a special guest, the only openly gay mayor in the Midwest, the mayor of South Bend, Indiana, Pete Buttigieg!"

At this point, not many people outside of South Bend knew who Pete was, so the reception of that announcement was, shall we say, lackluster. But, amongst the LGBTQ in the group, there was definitely some buzz of excitement.

Then, the next announcement took the wind out of my sails. Remember when I mentioned that this event would be the most beneficial if it was the only event in town that night? Well ...

The Tampa municipal primary elections were taking place in March of 2019, about five months after the normal general mid-term elections. A very wealthy local philanthropist by the name of David Straz (his name is on the giant Performing Arts Center in downtown Tampa) decided he was running for mayor, and he had a staffer at the DEC meeting.

"David Straz is having his campaign kickoff event at the Tampa Museum of Art this Friday, the 7th, also at 5:30 p.m. And it's open bar!" his staffer announced.

Shit.

Now, all the "normal Democrats" – the ones who can donate $50-$100 (AKA the bread and butter of any local campaign) would be shifting their focus to the open bar night at the museum. Looks like now my event would have to go for quality over quantity. At this point, we'd be lucky to break even on cost. Shit. And may I say that yet again with emphasis? *Shit!*

My poor wife had to listen to me whine on the car ride home, and then listen to the same whining when I called Bryan to fill him in on what happened that night. Then, we both had to listen to Bryan whining about the conflicting event schedules and how he was going to "rip someone a new one" (Don't worry; he didn't rip anybody any new anything although I'm sure he got some satisfaction from saying that.)

The next few days were spent preparing for the event and chasing attendees and donors. Finally, the day of the big show arrived and my nerves started tingling before noon. So many different things could go wrong, and every single one was playing itself out in my head. What if Pete's flight was delayed? Or canceled? What if no one showed up? Even though the event was indoors, what if it rained – people tended to stay home if the weather was bad. What if, what if, what if ...

The actual fundraiser wasn't going to start until 5:30 p.m., but I arrived at the venue at 4:00 – there was a lot to do – and Christie had been feeling ill all day. "Adam Hattersley for State House" signs and banners needed posting, the room needed to be set up, palm cards (4" x 9" pieces of campaign literature) needed arranging, and the check-in and all-important donation station had to be placed outside the doors. When that was finished, after about 20 minutes (I guess there wasn't that much to do, especially when moving fast with nervous energy), all I had left to do was wait around stewing, alone. And, yeah, watch a light rain start to fall (bad sign). *Shit.*

Thankfully, Christie (now feeling a bit better) arrived just past 5 p.m. and one of our volunteers shortly after (good signs!). Now with a campaign volunteer ready to handle the check-in desk, and my superstar wife, the event was ready to begin. All we needed was people to show up, and of course, Mayor Pete. Luckily, just about then I received a text from Bryan; he was at the airport, and Pete was off the plane headed his way, ETA about 45 minutes. Yes! That was almost perfect timing – hopefully by then the room would be, shall we say, less empty, and ready for his grand entrance.

The rain began to let up, and the clock inched closer to the official start time. The bartender arrived to finalize his preparations, and the photographer got to the venue exactly at the agreed upon time of 5:15 p.m. We. Were. Set.

Attendees began showing up right about 5:30 p.m.: most of the leadership of the county LGBTQ Caucus, two Tampa City Councilmen, our two DNC members and several others. I was beyond relived that people were arriving. The quality over quantity work-around plan due to the competing (and open bar) event less than three miles away seemed to be working. Mayor Rick Kriseman of St. Petersburg and his family walked in about 10 minutes to 6:00 – things were looking up! People were chatting, had drinks in their hands and were happily snacking on heavy hors d'oeuvres. The room was filling up in anticipation of the guest of honor's arrival.

If you've never been to a political fundraiser, they pretty much follow a formula. People show up usually in a half-hour window from the event's official start time. Mingling, snacks and chatting go on for about 30-45 minutes to let the crowd grow and settle in, then there is a "formal" program. One or two introductory speakers, a guest speaker (if you are going to have one), the candidate, and a "closer" who asks for additional donations. Tried and true, it works. Our agenda followed this template. The mingling and chatting portions were going well with about 35 people in the room when Bryan's car pulled up and he and Mayor Pete came inside. Honestly, I was a little surprised that he made it! Nearly two months of planning between almost a dozen people logistically paid off in that moment; now all that remained was the comparatively easy part of running the program.

The two Tampa DNC members (Alma Gonzalez and Alan Clendenin) took the stage to get everyone's attention and begin "the show." They spoke briefly, talking about how important state legislative races are (very much so!), and how we as Democrats finally had a shot at winning this seat after over 20 years of trying and failing. They did a great job and finished their portion of the program by announcing Mayor Kriseman, who would speak before introducing Mayor Pete.

Mayor Kriseman spoke passionately about his eight years in the State House before becoming St. Petersburg's Mayor. The rigor and responsibility of the job, and how I was more than up to the task. He talked about his city, and how far they had come from when he was elected, from being a relatively mediocre Florida town, to a world-recognized leading Clean City and its advancements in climate sustainability. He really painted a great picture of how having the right leadership with a motivated and caring agenda can benefit a community. Then, he started talking about Mayor Pete, who he had known for several years. Seen as a "rising star" in the National Democratic Party, as well as innovatively revitalizing a thought-dead Midwestern city. Pete had (and still has) a heck of a lot going for him and has an incredibly bright future. (Which became even more obvious in 2021 when he was sworn in as the Secretary of Transportation.)

Pete took the stage and gave a remarkably eloquent 10-minute speech – connecting his military service to mine, his values and mine, and how the country needs people like the two of us in leadership positions. He addressed how the next generation is ready, willing, and able to take up the mantle of social justice to ensure the United States moves forward to an equal and prosperous future for all its citizens, and that I was a key to that in Florida. Keep in mind that at this point, he and I had only spoken for about five minutes right when he arrived at the event. Suffice it to say, he was already an experienced veteran at political events and giving speeches like this. The people in the crowd didn't know what hit them, especially since most of them hadn't even known who Pete was before that point. They certainly knew who he was after that 10 minutes.

Toward the end of his talk, he introduced me (it was my event, after all), and I joined him on stage. The people there *really* liked what Pete had to say and let me tell you... *that* was a tough act to follow. Being a relative novice in the world of political speaking, I gave a somewhat unplanned (mistake) version of my slipshod (another mistake) stump speech, and quickly gave the mic back to Mayor Kriseman for the donation ask. Bottom line, I pretty much blew it (according to my wife, I was "terrible"). Fortunately, I wasn't really the person anyone was there to see, so the fundraising portion of the night didn't suffer.

The last half-hour or so of these events mirrors the first half-hour – drinking, eating, and schmoozing. Pete was *very* popular, and every single person from the LGBTQ Caucus never got more than five feet from him. He was extremely gracious and spent time with everyone who wanted to chat. Toward the end of our time at the venue, we devised a plan to gather some of the "bigger" people who had attended to go to dinner with Pete at one of Tampa's best steak houses, Council Oaks, at the Seminole Hard Rock Casino. We settled on a party of 12 for dinner (which we all chipped in to pay for since it wasn't an official campaign event, so therefore we couldn't use campaign funds).

Even though I kind of (really) botched my part of the program, Christie and I quickly gathered up all the campaign gear and rushed home feeling pretty good about ourselves. Ultimately, the event was a success, and now we had the opportunity to have dinner with Mayor Pete! We dumped everything at the house, including my tie, and called an Uber to take us to the casino (there was wine to drink in a relaxed atmosphere, so we didn't want to worry about driving, and I have a personal rule that I will not drive even after one drink). We were all meeting around 8 p.m., and without a reservation, we didn't know how long it would take to get a table.

We got to the restaurant and heard a group in the bar, and sure enough, it was our party. Besides Pete and my wife and I, we were joined by my consultant Bryan and his husband, our digital strategy guy Chris, DNC member Alan Clendenin, DNC member Alma Gonzales and her husband and their son, (who was the North Florida Labor Council president) and the former president of the Hillsborough County Young Democrats. A pretty good group if I do say so myself. We had plenty of time to get to know everyone since we ended up waiting quite a long time for a table large enough for our group. What do you do while waiting for a table in a swanky steak house? Have a few drinks, of course, which made the waiting period very enjoyable even though the wait took two hours, believe it or not.

We were finally shown to our table, and on the way, this lovely older couple jumped up and stopped us with cries of "Mayor Pete! Mayor Pete!" It turns out they were visiting Tampa, but in fact, were residents of South Bend, Indiana, and they loved Pete! He stopped to talk with them about their shared hometown and how things were there, where the town was headed, and what was on the horizon for them in the next few years. It was a great lesson in retail politics; always take time to talk to people who want to talk to you. Meeting someone face to face has such an enormous impact compared to literally every other method of political communication. Even if those folks didn't like Pete before meeting him, they certainly did after. They were, and will be, Pete voters for the rest of their lives.

So, now we settled in at the table for what would turn into a three-hour culinary marathon, which, to this day, is still one of the best dining experiences I've ever had in my life. Handmade butter with the bread, amazing appetizers, and interesting drinks – in fact, our digital guy, Chris, ordered this weird, smoke-infused Old Fashioned for Pete that came under a cake dish (you know the kind that you find at breakfast places that specialize in pie) which was filled with actual wood smoke – and no, Pete didn't even end up drinking it!

Conversation ranged all over the place, but two topics in particular stand out in memory. First off, my wife, Christie, who has been in sales most of her professional life and who swears by a method called "SPIN" selling, ended up giving the table a thorough description (more of a lecture) on this topic. In fact, according to her, it is a method that can and should be used in any type of persuasion activity – especially politics.

***

Comments from Christie:

If anyone knows me, they know I've been in sales for almost 20 years, and I love talking about it. I love everything about customer engagement, the roller coaster of emotions and the sales process. Several years ago, I worked for an events company that used a very well-known sales method called SPIN selling. They made me read a book by Neil Rackham and conducted extensive, and at times, aggressive, training on the process. I was also told I was horrible at it because it was the type of company that liked to tell their reps that they were terrible at sales (and everything else) even if you really were the top salesperson.

I was selling event sponsorships which are essentially packages to connect businesses with their target audiences so that was what most of my training was focused around. The method uses Situation, Problem, Implication, and Need-Payoff questioning to evaluate the gap between where your client is and where they want to be. It works best when you have a desired outcome or solution to sell.

So, for instance, if you're a politician, you want to ask your constituents' questions. Find out the implications of what is causing their problems — not just the surface issues and then offer them hope. Most often, it's values, freedom, rights, health, time, or money. It's everything that is super personal, and politicians usually don't ask enough questions. They do way too much preaching instead. My point of this rant was to get everyone thinking about what questions we were not asking. Why are we talking about issues without talking about the implications of these issues? Once you, as the politician, identifies these implications, you can develop a plan to bridge these gaps and get them (your constituents) to where they want to be. Without understanding this concept, we're pretty much just throwing ideas against the wall and hoping they stick.

✳✳✳

Interestingly enough, the person most rapt by this and asking the most questions was Pete. Here's another lesson in in-person politics: don't pretend to listen to people, actually listen and engage with them. Not only do you learn new things, but the person you're listening to feels important, appreciated, and heard. That impression goes a long way (especially in politics) because most people simply want to be heard by their elected leaders. And as Maya Angelou so famously said, "I've learned that people will forget what you said, people will forget what you did, but people will never forget how you made them feel." When people feel heard, they are more apt to buy into your ideas and to you as a politician.

The second major topic of conversation was the recent pick of our Democratic nominee for governor in Florida and his choice of running mate. Andrew Gillum was the progressive mayor of Tallahassee that wasn't polling very well in the five-way primary the week before, however, he was able to pull out an upset win with just over 34% of the vote. He waited until after the Republican nominee announced his selection of running mate (a former state representative and Hispanic woman from South Florida named Jeanette Nuñez – he honestly couldn't have picked better). Gillum's "big" announcement for his running mate was Chris King, one of the unexciting white guys that lost the primary. (*Chris, if you're reading this, sorry – and please keep in mind, we have nothing against you, you're really a great guy, just not very exciting*). My wife and I were watching the announcement live a few days before and as soon as the name was said, Christie looked at me and said simply, "We just lost the governor's race – all he had to do was pick a woman, literally any woman, and he had it in the bag." She wasn't wrong, and she said that exact thing at the table.

Our digital guy, "our" Chris, was of the opinion that the Democratic pick for Lieutenant Governor was a great one – and of course Christie, who was seated in the next chair, immediately turned on him.

"Why don't you like women?" she asked. Keep in mind, Chris is in no way against women; Christie sometimes likes to use hyperbole to rile people up (and she especially enjoys riling Chris up).

"What?" Chris asked, shock coming through in his voice. "I don't hate women!"

"Then why shouldn't Gillum have picked a female running mate? Aren't we supposed to be the inclusive party? Now we're going to lose independent women, and we're going to lose the governor's race flat out."

"I think Gillum picked the person closest to his own progressive ideology, what's wrong with that?" Chris retorted.

"You see, everyone? We lose these races because we are stupid. Pick for strategy, pick to win! And for God's sake, give a woman a chance!" Christie was nearly shouting at this point. "We can't make any changes if we don't win! And if we don't win, Florida is going to keep going down the far-right, conservative rabbit hole that it's been going down since the Republicans took power 20 years ago! Doesn't that bother you at all?" The Florida House, Senate and Governor's mansion had been in Republican control continuously since 1998, and Florida state laws had been going more "corporate" (conservative) ever since.

"Of course, it bothers me, but I don't think Gillum made that bad of a choice."

"Well, you're an idiot then. Every woman I've spoken to is upset, and he's lost more votes than he realizes. After Gillum won the primary, I *actually* thought we might have a chance since he excites the base so much, but after his pick for running mate – he's screwed himself and the entire state of Florida."

"It was a dumb pick, Chris – she's right," I said. There were several echoes of that sentiment from around the table.

"Well, I still think he'll be okay," Chris murmured, unwilling (or unable) to admit he may not have thought his position through thoroughly.

Now everyone around the table was not only talking about the governor's race, but the strategy (or lack thereof) behind campaign decisions. Because, when it comes right down to it, if you don't win, you can't make any changes. We must play to win, and that's exactly what the opposition had been doing for two decades in Florida and it was obviously working, so why hadn't we learned that lesson? Just because your opponent is using a particular tactic, that doesn't make it a bad tactic.

Ultimately, there were several big takeaways from this whole experience. Let's do this in list form:

- You may have connections your never knew about; explore them
- Listen, learn, and make people feel heard
- Don't argue with my wife when she's right

Note: In case you were wondering, after paying for flights, hotel, food, a photographer, and everything else associated with the Mayor Pete event, and counting all of the contributions we received for it, we ended up losing about $150 on the whole endeavor. Financially a bad deal, but man, what a great experience and well worth it.

Adam's fundraising total: $43,621
Joe's fundraising total: $102,827

CHAPTER SEVENTEEN

Me Too No More

Amanda Murphy, Dianne Hart, Phil Hornback, Jason Marlow, Christie, Amy Bolick
and Bryan Farris behind Adam at the "Me Too No More" press conference in Tampa

Photo used with courtesy of the Hattersley Family

Chapter 17:

Me Too No More

It was now late September, and we are getting down to crunch time. Forums, events, meetings, interviews, and fundraising (or lack thereof) were all-consuming now. We were looking for any opportunity to get my name and message out, especially if it was low cost. The "golden egg" is big bang-for-the-buck stuff: radio interviews, large events, and if we were lucky, getting my face on TV. As luck would have it, one of those golden opportunities came along.

There was an event for educators in my district to meet with local candidates, and most of the people on the ballot within 30 miles were there (including one of our statewide candidates) – it was the place to be that night. The event was fairly typical. Each candidate introduced themselves briefly—from the school board all the way to congressional candidates—but the event's real objective was to get to know the local movers and shakers within the (substantial) teachers' union. All that is beside the point, except for one brief conversation I had with Jason Marlow, who was the campaign manager from another candidate's campaign.

Jason hadn't been in this part of Florida for very long but was a long-time Floridian (including multiple degrees from Florida State University). He was running the campaign for the State House candidate (Phil Hornback) in District 58 just north of me. Phil was, and is, a great guy – a union brick layer turned teacher, with a heart of gold. His only problem: he was running in a ruby red part of the county, and sadly, he had nearly zero chance of winning his race, and he knew it.

Jason told me that a small polling and strategy group called Bold Blue was helping Florida's Democratic candidates, and they had reached out to Phil that day. They were trying to get a TV news segment done on their efforts to turn the state blue. They asked if Phil wanted to get some free TV airtime, and oh by the way, did Phil know any other local candidates who may be interested as well? He wanted to gauge my interest because, after all, this TV thing may not even happen (Bold Blue was still trying to pitch their story idea to the local station), but either Jason or Phil would call me in the next few days if anything solidified. Bold Blue was making this pitch for two reasons. First, to get Democrats elected, but more importantly, to show that their group was an influential player in Florida politics. If they could successfully accomplish both objectives, they would have plenty of business in future election cycles. But for now, they were doing a lot of work— good work—at very reasonable rates. We would later find out that the day rate was the best we could hope for—free!

The next day, Phil called me. "Are you available tomorrow morning? This Bold Blue TV thing is a go, and they want two of us. It's going to be around 10 a.m. at the county party office."

This turned out to be perhaps the biggest favor another candidate did for me during the entire election. Can I meet you at the local Democratic party office tomorrow morning to get free TV airtime? You bet your ass I can.

I told Bryan about the opportunity, and he planned to meet me there. Phil's campaign manager, Jason Marlow, who first told me about the media opportunity, would be there as well. So, the two candidates, two campaign staffers, two Bold Blue representatives, and the two people from the TV station met the next day. That's it – a nice, small group.

The story itself was very straightforward. The main interviewee was the head of Bold Blue, and Phil and I were there as "local flavor," so to speak – local candidates getting value out of Bold Blue's efforts. Although until this, neither Phil nor I had gotten anything out of their efforts yet. But we understood what they were trying to do, their ideas, and where they wanted to go. When the reporter asked if one of the candidates wanted to make an on-camera comment, once again, Phil came in clutch, "Adam, why don't you do it?" Clutch. Phil is such an amazing and thoughtful human being.

Believe it or not, this part of the story isn't that important either. This background is though, because it sets up what happens next. The second Bold Blue staffer there was a guy name Tony Panaccio, and he had a personal pet cause that he wanted to get into the greater political conversation. It's actually a huge cause, and extremely worthy of legislative action, but Florida being Florida, nothing had happened on the topic at our Capitol in decades. The subject: sexual assault and how survivors are treated by the criminal justice system. Unbeknownst to me, Tony had been bending Bryan's ear about his ideas the entire morning, and they had both been watching how Phil and I spoke on camera. I didn't know if it was Bryan's suggestion, or if I just happened to be more "on" that day, but Tony wanted to pitch his ideas to me to see if I would run with them. Using Bold Blue's resources and their local media contacts, this could be a pretty big thing (according to him). He got Bryan's buy-in to convince me to hear him out.

The next day, Bryan gave me a call.

"So, the other guy at the DEC office yesterday, Tony, has an idea that he thinks would be perfect for you and the campaign," Bryan told me.

"Oh, yeah? What's that?" I asked.

"He wants to bring Florida into the 21st century regarding how we treat sexual assault victims. He was hoping we could meet him at the Bold Blue offices in St. Petersburg later this week to discuss it. I feel like this could be the home run we've been trying to hit. What do you think?"

"Well, we have nothing to lose, might as well hear him out. It sounds like a cause worth fighting for. Let's set it up."

The next morning, I met Bryan at a small house a few blocks away from St. Pete's Tropicana Field that Bold Blue was using for an office. Tony and his boss, Madison, (who we had met while taping the TV spot) were excited to talk to us and hoped we had most of that day to work on their initiative, which was rather surprising since I hadn't even agreed to be a part of it yet. Tony was sure I would be on board though, and he spent the next hour describing the background and details of his idea. Tony called it "Me Too No More," in recognition of the "Me Too" movement that was gaining momentum all over the country.

Statistics showed that although nearly one out of every five American women will be sexually assaulted at some point in their lives, barely six out of every 1,000 suspected rapists will ever see the inside of a prison cell. Some research had also shown that upwards of nine out of every 10 sexual assaults go unreported, and in eight out of 10 cases, the victims of sexual assault know their assailants. Suffice it to say, these numbers were terrifying. This was (and still is) an issue that deserves to be confronted, and the victims deserve someone fighting for them. This was now much more than just a press opportunity for me – it became central to my goals as a prospective legislator. Later that evening when I was discussing the topic with Christie, she was adamant that I needed to do this (although I had already committed myself to the cause earlier in the day).

Tony wanted to propose aggressive (for Florida) legislative reform on the issue of sexual assault that would go a long way in protecting victims. It was a three-part plan that over a dozen states had already implemented:

1. Eliminate the large backlog of rape kits in the state by mandating (and funding) better and more efficient DNA testing regulations

2. Incorporate specialized training for interviewing officers known as the "Forensic Experiential Trauma Interview" (FETI) technique which stops treating victims like perpetrators and has been proven more effective in obtaining

an accurate account of events, while not re-traumatizing victims.

3. Eliminate the statute of limitations for felony sex crimes

Tony then laid out his plan for media coverage for the initiative (with me out in front), including print, digital and a TV press conference. He had even been working on a speech for a few months while they looked for a candidate to pitch their idea to. He envisioned an approximately 10-12-minute live press conference in front of the county courthouse with dozens of activists and other candidates standing behind me in support.

Compared to what I had been doing throughout the campaign, this was a big deal. We were struggling to get any press coverage since most Florida politicos thought I didn't have a chance to win. "Me Too No More" could change everything. Not only that, the subject was one that I wanted to fight for. The numbers show that whether you're aware of it or not, you almost certainly know sexual assault victims, so this issue should be a personal one for all of us. After a brief aside with Bryan, we decided to take a swing. After all, these are the kind of issues that politicians *should* focus on.

Tony showed me a copy of the speech (he called it "congressional level" in scope) and wanted to spend the afternoon having me practice its delivery in front of our small group. They would give me pointers on tone, pacing, where to pause, what to emphasize and how to make a better impact with public speaking, all while polishing the content of the speech. The first run-through of the speech went okay. Tony called it a "five out of 10 but with definite potential." I'll take that. I knew I still had work to do, because in all reality, I wasn't the only one going out a limb. Bold Blue was, too, and we all wanted this to go as well as possible.

After a couple of hours, the delivery was up to at least a 7.5 out of 10, and I left their office with the homework assignment of practice, practice, practice. Practice in front of a mirror, practice in front of your wife, record yourself and watch the "game tape." Anything to improve. We weren't sure when the press conference would be, but I had to be ready on relatively short notice. This experience, and others, have ingrained in me that practicing public speaking (and specific speeches) is critical to a more believable and comfortable delivery. Don't be afraid to feel like an idiot standing in front of a mirror in your home giving a speech to no one. It's an important part of the process.

Two days after the St. Petersburg prep session, I received another call from Bryan.

"We have a date and time for the press conference! Tomorrow morning at 10 a.m. in front of the county courthouse. We'll have two or three TV stations there, so let's call all the other candidates to see who we can get to stand behind you in support," he told me. "I'll swing by the DEC office in the morning to get their lectern so we can look more official. Oh, and wear a purple tie to look bipartisan."

Tomorrow morning! Hoping I had practiced the speech enough, I gathered commitments from other candidates to join us for the conference. Phil Hornback, bless his soul, was in (and he promised to bring Jason Marlow, as well). So was Amanda Murphy, who was running for the State Senate in the neighboring county, and Dianne

Hart, who was running for the State House in District 61, just to the West of me. Every other person I called had conflicts. Every. Single. One. Thinking how weak and ridiculous it would look to have only four people "supporting" this great initiative (and how not-so-great it would imply the idea to be), I called one of our super-volunteers, Amy Bolick, to see if she could make an appearance. She was *crushing* our field program, and we wanted to keep her as involved as we could because we knew she had the potential to impact the race. Adding her and my wife would give us a good half-dozen folks standing behind me in the morning. That would help fill the camera shot for the TV stations.

When the time came, we drove downtown, arriving about 90 minutes before our scheduled showtime. We still had to set up the lectern, some campaign signage, our own digital cameras and microphones, and coordinate with the TV news crews so we could start at 10 a.m. Being nervous, I didn't realize that 90 minutes was *way* too early – Bryan wouldn't get there with the lectern until about 9:40 a.m. – so we had nearly an hour to kill. Luckily, there was a coffee shop about two blocks away where we could wait (and where I could get increasingly more nervous), as I continued to review the speech. Drinking two cups of coffee in quick succession (while already on edge) was probably not the best idea because by the time Bryan called to say he was about to unload the lectern, my hands were shaking.

We headed back to the courthouse just in time to meet Bryan as he (almost) skidded to an illegal stop at the curb, shouting for us to help him unload the lectern from his car before he got arrested. Mere seconds later and that near disaster averted, Bryan drove off to find parking while my wife and I set things up. I had to do some quick "Southern engineering" using two wire coat hangers to get my campaign sign "attached" to the front of the lectern before anyone noticed how fast and loose we were playing. Regardless of the initial chaos, we were ready by the time the two camera crews arrived.

The sound engineers from both stations set their microphones on the lectern, and I was wearing a third mic for our own sound capture. This was starting to look like a real press conference! My half-dozen supporters had taken their positions, and the TV crews signaled that they were rolling. Bryan approached the lectern.

"I would like to introduce Adam Hattersley, Democratic candidate for State House District 59, who will be making a statement. He will be available for your questions after his remarks." Here we go.

I approached the lectern, opened my binder with the speech inside, took a deep breath, and went into the next 11 minutes with an outward confidence masking my inner trepidation.

"Good morning and thank you all for coming out today. There are moments in American history which transcend our national conversations and political discourse and offer us the ability to reveal truth..."

Despite fighting the wind to keep my speech from blowing off the lectern, the press conference was surprisingly smooth. The TV crews were only there to tape the event, so they didn't have any questions after I was done; they simply packed up and went on to their next assignment. My wife, though, was touched a bit more.

"Things like *this* are why people should get into politics," she said. She honestly got a little teary-eyed, not because of me or what I had said, but from the gravity of the topic. Several of her close friends are victims themselves, and not one had seen justice.

Always ready to break any tense or emotional moments, Bryan nearly shouted to our small group — "I'm parked five blocks away, and we have to get this lectern out of here before we get a ticket! Is anyone closer with a car big enough for this thing?"

Yes, yes, someone *was* closer, the candidate. Christie ran to get our car and nearly jumped the curb in front of us so we could hastily load the car, and off we drove to the county Democratic office to return the lectern. Adrenaline high successfully quashed, we drove off still feeling like we had just done a good thing.

Ultimately, my goal that day was not just to deliver a press conference to a bunch of supporters or even to the media. The goal was to do such a great job that I actually won this election and could then affect real change by introducing and passing this bill and others that were just as important. It is a heavy responsibility to legislate. One, I think, candidates rarely realize. Candidates go out and talk a lot. And I mean A LOT. They want to fix healthcare, education, transportation... they speak in generalities and make campaign promises that will mostly never be kept. I didn't want to be *that* guy. I wanted to be the guy that talked about actual issues and proposed legislation to fix those issues – not in generalities but with precise solutions. I wanted to be the guy who could heal some of our division and change things for the better. Maybe I was an idealist, maybe I was a bit naïve, but isn't that what government is supposed to do? I didn't actually know how to do that until this opportunity came along. Campaigning and legislating are *very* different animals, and that day was the first time I spoke as though I were a lawmaker instead of just a candidate.

I learned a lot from this experience, but probably the most important thing was that when given the opportunity to fight for something worth fighting for, you go all in. Be the idealist. We need them.

Adam's fundraising total: $49,565

Joe's fundraising total: $137,577

Note: The complete text of the speech is in the appendix. I would strongly encourage you to read it to see an example of a well-crafted, legislation-focused speech.

CHAPTER EIGHTEEN

Local Visibility

Volunteers building large Hattersley signs
Photo used with courtesy of the Hattersley Family

Chapter 18:
Local Visibility

I've discussed the endorsement process before, but I want to highlight an especially critical endorsement: the newspaper of record in your area. For me, that was the *Tampa Bay Times*, one of the largest and most widely read newspapers in Florida. The *Times* has a storied history dating back to 1884, and it is the creator of PolitFact. com and its fabled "Truth-O-Meter" (a project that led to a Pulitzer Prize in 2009). Their endorsement (or lack of) is the statement in Central Florida on a race and can usually be counted on to sway thousands of votes in a district. In my neck of the woods, the *Times* is the "big dog."

"I'm not leaving this one to chance," Bryan said when he called me to discuss the *Times* endorsement. "After you write out your questionnaire answers, I'm going to have an expert look at them before we submit anything."

"An expert? At what?" I asked.

"I always have this guy look over my client's *Times* questionnaires and give them a primer on what to expect for the interview. He's never let me down. Getting the Times behind you will go a long way toward winning this thing. You already have an advantage, too," Bryan explained.

"How do you mean, an advantage?"

"The Times already interviewed Joe during the primary, and they don't interview twice – they'll go off his answers from August. You, on the other hand, will be fresh in their minds and will have that rosy and recent glow. Definitely an advantage in my book," he told me. "Have you started on your questionnaire?"

"I'm just about done with it," I told him.

"Good. When you're finished, print it out and bring it with you when you meet my "*Times* Whisperer," he'll also walk you through a practice interview. Take notes when he does!" Bryan told me before clicking off the line.

A few days later, I found myself in a boutique coffee shop in Ybor City called the Blind Tiger. It has a very cozy, post-hipster vibe that caters to the young and fashionable crowd and was the *Times* Whisperer's (I'll call him "T.W.") favorite hang-out spot. Not exactly the dark, smoke filled, backroom setting that political movies tell us a meeting like this should take place in. Another cinematic preconception shattered.

Truthfully, the meeting's beginning was a bit awkward. I simply sat across a table from T.W., quietly sipping my designer coffee while he spent nearly half an hour pouring over my written responses while making edits. He didn't even look up when I went to the barista for a refill. Suddenly, he put his pen down and spoke for the first time since sitting down.

"Why do you want to be a state representative?" he asked.

I gave my usual, if somewhat unrehearsed, response. He cut me off halfway through.

"You have to be crisper than that. More confident. *Sell me!*" he said.

We went through that exercise on each of his questions, not moving on until he was satisfied that my answers were strong (and concise) enough for his liking. I was in interview bootcamp.

When he was pleased with my "coached-up" verbal performance, we went over his notes on my written portion of the process. It was positively uncanny how closely his notes transformed my meandering answers into near copies of what we just went over in spoken form. No wonder Bryan referred to him as the Whisperer – he was in my head before I was! The intense two hours I spent with T.W. may have been some of the most productive time since I filed to be on the ballot.

Armed with T.W.'s notes and a promise to continue practicing my answers in front of a mirror (yes, it actually helps), I felt much better prepared for my in-person interview the next week at the *Times* building. T.W. told me to expect a panel-style interview in front of four to five people from the paper's political and editorial staff that should clarify my now-improved written positions from the questionnaire. I was ready.

The day arrived, and I dressed in my best (only) suit for the interview. I was nervous and left even earlier than normal to make sure I could find parking and navigate the huge *Times* Building. All went smoothly, though, and I found myself in a dimly lit and almost empty newsroom well ahead of schedule (yes, again). The first person I found was the *Times* military reporter, so we chatted about our respective service experiences while he sent an assistant to let the political staff know I had arrived.

A few minutes later, the assistant returned with the political editor in tow.

"Welcome to the *Times*, thanks for coming in. It's just you and me today, so let's head to the conference room and get started," he said.

I had been expecting a panel interview, but the gods seemed to be in my favor. A one-on-one interview is typically less formal and more conversational, provided you can establish a good rapport. I took advantage of the walk through the newsroom to strike up a friendly conversation to help ease us into a more favorable mood for when the actual interview started. Small talk can go a long way to getting someone on your side and is just another tool in the toolbox.

The interview only lasted about 20 minutes, and closely mirrored the practice that T.W. put me through. We started with the expected questions:

"Tell me about yourself."

"Why are you running?"

"What are your top priorities?"

The final question is one that every candidate needs to be carefully prepared for. The answer you give should be well practiced, especially after using it while trying to convince people to invest in your campaign. This is the topic used to determine if you get support or don't. And if there is one question that is most important to people like the person sitting across from me, it is:

"What is your path to victory?"

The interviewer was asking me to convince him that not only did I have a shot to win, but that I was the only one who could. No one likes to back a losing horse, so it was up to me to describe how I would cross the finish line first. What had changed since the last election that now makes the race winnable for me? Why was I a better candidate than my opponent? I used every arrow in my quiver.

Unfortunately for me, however, by the time the interview was over, I did not have a read on which side the *Times* endorsement would fall. I felt good about my "performance," but sometimes objective news organizations will simply put their money on who *they* think will win instead of who aligns better with their values. I knew that I was certainly in danger of losing the endorsement based on nothing other than history and fundraising, and that weighed heavily on my mind when I called Bryan from the car.

"Hah-llllllooo?" he answered in his usual fashion. "How'd it go?"

"I think it went really well. They said the endorsements will come out in about three weeks, but I'm still worried they don't think I have a chance, so they will go with Joe just to hedge their bets," I said.

"Nah, you're such a good candidate, I can't imagine they won't go with you," he said, sounding very upbeat. "There's nothing more you can do now about it, anyway, so put it out of your mind."

"Good advice. What's next on the list?" I asked.

"Well, have you seen those giant eight-foot versions of political signs? It's time to order some for you! I've already found a few places that will let us put them up. We need to get about 10 of them – that work for you?"

"Those giant, gaudy things on the side of the road? Hell, yeah!" I was wondering when this particular political rite-of-passage was coming.

"Great! I'll get that going. It only takes a few days, so you have to find someone with a truck to pick them up. Oh, and buy a bunch of wood to make frames," Bryan reminded me.

Fortunately, I'm an engineer. My signs would be able to withstand a hurricane. The rest of the ride home had me figuring out the best way to design a sturdy and indestructible structure to hold my enlarged name for the world to see. A task for the candidate themselves? Probably not – but this task was definitely in my wheelhouse.

Garage Full of Signage

There's an old political adage that says, "signs don't vote." That's very true. There is little data regarding what, if any, impact yard signs or other signage has on an election. But be damned if any campaign doesn't have hundreds (or thousands) of signs all over their district during election season. Have candidates lent overinflated importance and attention to yard signs? Yes. Knowing this, was I still excited for giant "Adam Hattersley" signs? Damn straight I was!

I had my sign frame design all set and just needed the materials and a friend with a truck to help. Fellow Navy veteran and local artist Bryant Martinez volunteered to meet me at the hardware store with his pickup, and we loaded it with 50 eight-foot, pressure-treated two-by-fours, wood screws and roofing nails. Overkill? Maybe. Fun construction project and minor diversion? Certainly.

After unloading our hardware and lumber haul, Bryant drove off to pick up the now ready giant signs, and I set to work on a prototype frame. By the time Bryant returned, my garage had been taken over by a wooden monster, waiting to be copied another nine times. We attached one sign to the frame to complete the first iteration and stacked the remaining placards along the edge of the garage so there was room for more construction. Unfortunately, Bryant had another engagement and had to go, but his help put me well on my way.

I forgot to mention that Christie was out running some errands that morning and wasn't expecting the disaster area of a garage when she got home. It's one thing to describe what ended up being an eight-foot by eight-foot creation is, but a whole other thing to see it in real life. To put it mildly, she was not happy.

"How many of these are you making?" she asked.

"There will be 10 total when I'm done," I told her.

"And where are they going to live until you put them up?"

It was a good question, and one that I probably should have thought about ahead of time. There just wasn't room for 10 of these things in our garage.

"I was only going to make the first one, to start. The rest won't be built until we're ready to set them up." I said, trying to recover for my unusual lack of planning. Turns out, that was a good plan, albeit completely impromptu.

I had just been so excited to get going on the new signs that I didn't think any further than that.

"Okay," she said. "At least get some help; I don't want you killing yourself with these things."

Once more, she was right. The sign was both heavy and awkward, not a good combination. Not to mention that I was going to have to rent a trailer just to drive these things to their final destinations. Maybe I should have built them on-site where they were going, but I had let my enthusiasm get the better of me. Regardless of my excitement, these tasks normally don't fall to the candidate themselves. Paid campaign managers and field staff usually handled non-fundraising items like the one I found myself engrossed in, but seeing as I couldn't afford a paid campaign manager or field staff, it was down to me to perform nearly all of my campaign's functions. I had to be scrappy and flexible. Fortunately, being scrappy and flexible was also in my wheelhouse.

I decided to put off building the remaining signs to the weekend, and conscripted a couple of my neighbors, Amy, her wife, and her father-in-law to assist. With a team, we could complete the other nine signs quickly and install them all in one day. When lacking paid staffers, the next best thing is finding volunteers. I love it when a good plan comes together.

That Sunday morning, my neighbors Nick and Martin, as well as Amy and her family, gathered at my house bright and early. I was providing coffee and donuts, and they were graciously giving up their Sunday. We got a little assembly line set up and were able to finish the signs with (surprisingly) no incident or injury.

Alongside her canvassing and field planning, Amy had arranged our schedule for sign installation that day. Her father-in-law and I rented a trailer for his truck, and we loaded up. I threw a bunch of tools and a post-hole digger in with the signs and off we went to the first location. It took nearly an hour to figure out the best way to put one of these monstrosities up, but we learned a lot of lessons for the rest of the day. Ten stops and some pizza later, my district had 10 new, eye-popping political signs. Victory!

At least I thought it was a victory, until two days later when my campaign website got several messages saying one of our large signs was blocking the view of an intersection.

Shit.

These signs were huge, and I couldn't move one on my own. I needed to fix the problem quickly, so I called the closest person I had to a staffer, Amy Bolick. She already had the sign installation experience from the weekend, so she was the logical person to ask for help. Luckily, she had some time and said she would meet me at the location.

I pulled up to the intersection where our problematic sign stood, and only had to wait a few minutes for Amy to arrive, and she had brought her wife along. Good news since an extra person would make the move that much easier. Bad news though; it had started raining. A simple task was quickly turning into a messy slog. Undeterred, we set to work, and rehomed the sign with only getting slightly (majorly) muddy. We were even able to do some drive-by tests to make sure the view of the intersection was clear.

On my way home, Bryan called and said he was going to meet me at my house. A little unusual, but he said he was on my side of town, and we should take advantage of the opportunity to catch up. Sounded good, a little strategy catch-up and fine-tuning is never a bad thing. He was waiting for me in front of the house when I drove up, looking at his phone with a big smile on his face.

"I have a surprise and a present for you!" he said as I got out of my car, mud still all over me. He showed me his phone, opened to the *Tampa Bay Times* website.

"The *Tampa Bay Times* recommends Adam Hattersley" the headline of the story read.

Holy shit. I got it.

Bryan reached into the back of his car while I was still reading the article, and fished out a large, triangular package.

"I was pretty confident you were going to get the endorsement, so I had these signs made in anticipation. We can tack them up in the corner of your giant signs and everyone will know that the *Times* is supporting you!" he said, taking one of the 10 placards out of the package. It read in large letters "Endorsed by the *Tampa Bay Times!*"

"This is amazing!" I said as we hugged it out. I felt like I was finally starting to get some momentum. "I'm already wet and muddy, I might as well go back out and get these up right away." My face fell a little at the prospect of going back into the elements, but the sooner I got those placards up the better.

I've discussed a lot of different qualities to foster during a campaign, but one often overlooked quality is tenacity. The ability to persevere and overcome. To find solutions and work strategically to make sure you get the desired outcome. Don't let something as banal as being underfunded deter you from what you need to do. Find a way, and if all else fails, do it yourself.

Adam's fundraising total: $56,524

Joe's fundraising total: $170,187

CHAPTER NINETEEN

Unexpected Surprises

Adam with former Vice President Joe Biden
Photo by Phil Hornback

Chapter 19:

Unexpected Surprises

There was now less than a month to Election Day, and our county Supervisor of Elections had, in fact, already sent out the "Vote by Mail" ballots to those who had requested them. Bottom line: people were voting. Right now. We were in the home stretch, but there was still so much to do, especially since the election's outcome was in no way clear to anyone. Our last-month plan and activities could still sway the election in our favor. Or not.

Discussing the current situation with Bryan and Chris, we determined that we would sink every dollar we could into digital advertising. It was the highest return on investment we had available to us, and we were going to squeeze it for all it was worth. Chris was able to precisely target the exact voters we needed and bombard them with my maize and blue ads, while at the same time, do larger but more infrequent ad blasts to our lower tier targets. With our bases covered as well as we could with digital, we still had backup plans for a direct mail piece or two and a small Spanish language radio spot if we could dredge up the resources. As my old Navy pilot buddies used to say, "Plan your flight and fly your plan."

Even though we had our communications scheduled and in place, we still needed extra help on the ground. Canvassing, texting and phone calls were becoming more important in chasing the Democratic base. No way around it, we needed more manpower, and at this point, there was really only one place to get it: the county party.

Thus far, my campaign had received exactly zero help from either the state or county parties. House District 59 was considered a lost cause and wasn't on any target list, and no one wanted to bet their money on a sinking ship. I understood that, and I have no hard feelings about it. It's politics, after all, and the larger Democratic organizations needed to put their money where they thought it would do the most good. Looking at the data, I would have made the same decision in their shoes.

Lucky for me, though, we were about to get a new piece of data. My campaign didn't have the money for polling (it was in the original $180,000 plan, but we were now working with a $60,000 plan; there had been a lot of cuts). Independently, the county party had decided to do some polling of their own, and had contacted Bold Blue – that's right, the same group that helped me with "Me Too No More" – and had them poll several races in the county (mine included) using their low-cost method.

"I just got off the phone with the County Party Chairwoman," Bryan told me during one of our now frequent phone conversations. "I've been trying to get them to help the campaign for months and had been hitting a brick wall until today. She has some news for us and was hoping we could stop by the party office tomorrow morning."

"I guess that's good news. Any help is better than the zero help we've had so far. I'll meet you there at about 10 a.m.?" I replied.

"That works for me. I wonder what they have up their sleeves?" Bryan said before hanging up.

We had gotten so used to relying on no one but ourselves, we had given up hope of any party intervention. Several of my "candidate circuit" friends had been on the receiving end of both state and county funding for months, and by this time, we had simply resolved to win the damn election on our own. Were my fortunes about to change? I didn't get my hopes up.

The next morning, I met Bryan for coffee and a quick catch-up before heading to the party office. I had been there a few times to drop off campaign literature in case any of their volunteers wanted to canvass in my district, but it was still mostly foreign territory to me. The party chairwoman greeted us warmly (even though she and Bryan do not get along) and ushered us into her office.

"I have good news!" she said. "I've been in contact with the state party, and they wanted to know if any races down here were close, so I had some polling done. You came back within one point of your opponent!"

"Holy shit! That's fantastic!" I exclaimed. We had closed nearly the entire gap from the last election and had done it alone and on a shoestring budget.

"It gets better," she continued. "With that kind of information, I might be able to get the state party to give you a little financial help. Until then, what can we do to help get you across the finish line?"

"Besides money, what we really need is a field director," Bryan told her.

"We have a super-volunteer helping us, you know Amy Bolick from the LGBTQ Caucus, but unless we can pay her something – anything – she can't take any more time off work to dedicate to us. We really need her, and she said if we could give her what she would lose by stepping back from her freelance work, it would go a long way toward guaranteeing at least 20 hours per week. I'm doing everything I can to find just $500," I added.

"Okay, we can definitely help with that. I'll run it by my finance committee, but I'm pretty sure I can get you $500 to pay her for the rest of the campaign. I should have a check for you tomorrow morning."

Great news, indeed! We were finally – *finally* – being taken seriously! I sure hoped that $500 for Amy was only a start to the support going into the final weeks of the campaign. Before we left, we got a little more hope on that front with the chairwoman's promise that she would use the positive polling results as leverage to get the big dogs from the state party involved too.

I called Amy on the way home with the good news.

"That's amazing!" she said. "I was hoping something might work out. I have been so excited; I even did some trial texting runs last night. I found a free program and was able to text 200 voters in an hour. Now that I'm on the payroll, I can spend a couple hours each night texting!"

Holy shit! Not only was Amy going to do research and run our field program, but she was able to directly contact 200 voters *in one hour*!? Output like that was worth far more than $500 for three weeks. Talk about high return on investment!

"I'm still digging into the last three election cycles' voter data but I'm getting a much clearer picture of how to attack the last weeks before Election Day," she continued. "I'll have lists for our volunteer canvassers ready for Saturday."

Every campaign needs an Amy. Even though it was late in the campaign season, I was extraordinarily fortunate to have found her.

Now armed with a paid campaign staffer, a tiny bit of party support, a robust plan, and a very encouraging poll, we felt like momentum was swinging our way for the first time since I signed my name on the filing papers seven months earlier. That morning certainly put a smile on my face.

Chance Encounter

The election was now 15 days away. In-person early voting was about to begin, and I was spending more time knocking on doors than ever before. I was finishing up a canvassing list that Amy had sent me when I got a phone call from a campaign circuit friend, Jason Marlow, the campaign manager for Phil Hornback who had already been generous with his time.

"I hear there's a big event at the University of South Florida this afternoon. A campaign rally with the gubernatorial nominee Andrew Gillum, U.S. Senator Bill Nelson, and their special guest, former Vice President Joe Biden! Want to meet Phil and I there and try to get in?" he said in an excited rush.

"That sounds great! Hopefully, we can get at least a glimpse of them. I'll meet you there."

Jason sent me the event details, and I got in my car to head over. The Secret Service needed to screen everyone attending the event, so we had to be in line at least two and a half hours ahead of the rally's start time.

Sweaty and dirty from my morning's canvassing and wearing my campaign t-shirt and my old submarine's ball cap, I met Jason near the rally site. By the time we arrived, the line to get in was already several hundred deep.

"Great, who knows if we'll even be able to make it inside," Jason said before calling Phil to let him know where we were in line. "Hopefully, this venue is big enough."

We kept our places within the barriers that had been erected to keep order and welcomed Phil when he got there 15 minutes later. We still had a long time to wait before the line would begin moving, and we chatted about our respective campaigns to while away the monotony. Phil was running in an even more hostile environment than I was, against a well-funded and well-liked incumbent, in a district that had favored Republicans for over 40 years. He still maintained a positive outlook though, and people couldn't help but feel better just by being around him. He's a great guy.

After 30 minutes, we saw some other familiar faces. Two more of our candidate friends were walking by on the VIP side of the barriers. Just like Phil and I, Deb and Debbie (no relation) were both running for state house seats, and we had all gotten to know each other over the last seven months. They saw us and stopped by to chat.

"What are you doing in line?" Deb asked.

"Waiting to get in, what else?" I said. "What are you doing over there?"

"You guys weren't invited? Both of us are on the pass list," Debbie told us.

Hold the phone. Invited? Pass list? I quickly identified the difference between the two Debs and Phil and I — "the Debs" were being supported by the state party (granted, not at an overwhelming level, but certainly a tangible one). Phil's and my districts were considered "lost causes," so not only was the state party refusing to help us, it "seemed" like they went out of their way to exclude us from any event that could be in the press. Fortunately, Debbie was having none of it.

"Come with us, they won't be able to turn you away once they know you're on the ballot," she said determinedly, and pulled us across the barrier.

The four of us walked up to the VIP check-in table, a few party staffers welcomed the Debs as we passed, and we got in the much shorter line with the other local politicos. One of the incumbent County Commissioners (who was on the list) also made a bit of a fuss on our behalf, and Phil and I were able to sneak into the event. We huddled up with the other candidates and elected officials in the very front row, right next to the stage for the nearly three-hour wait for the event to begin.

I don't know about Phil, but I was feeling exceedingly lucky to have not just gotten into the venue, but also placed at the front of the "rope line" that the stars of the show would greet the attendees from after the rally. Did it matter that I was a sweaty mess? Not anymore.

The longer we waited, the more people packed into the venue, and the higher the excitement level rose. Periodically, a campaign staffer for either Andrew Gillum or Bill Nelson would ask a candidate near me to come backstage to chat with them, or to even meet the former vice president. I wasn't important enough to warrant such an invitation, but that wasn't bothering me, especially since I (technically) wasn't supposed to even be this close to the action or in the room at all.

The crowd was starting to get impatient, when finally, someone walked out on stage and up to the microphone. It took me a second before I recognized her; it was Fentrice Driskell! Another friend from the campaign circuit, she was also running for a state house seat. The big difference was that she was being heavily supported by the state party, and was therefore expected to win her election. It made sense that the party wanted to put the spotlight on her, especially since the rally was being held in the district she was running to represent.

She did an amazing job, and was followed by an equally amazing speaker, the current Florida House Democratic Leader, Janet Cruz, who had been term limited out of the House but was running for a state senate seat in the Tampa area against a formidable incumbent. She was our party's best chance of flipping an all-important senate seat from Republican to Democratic control. She is a natural public speaker and was the perfect choice to get the crowd's excitement level to sky-high levels.

The best "warm-up" act was saved for last: U.S. Representative Kathy Castor. She had served Tampa in Congress for 12 years and was an outspoken advocate for not only her district, but the entire state of Florida.

Well-loved and well-respected, she held the rally goers' rapt attention during her brief remarks. The biggest response she received though, was when she introduced the trio that would share the stage for the main part of the rally.

"Please welcome to the stage the Democratic nominee for Governor, Andrew Gillum, U.S. Senator Bill Nelson, and the former Vice President of the United States, Joe Biden!"

The crowd went nuts!

After three hours of waiting, the people we had come to see finally took the stage. There were barstools for them to sit on and as they took their places, Senator Nelson headed to the microphone first. He regaled the crowd with stories of his time in the senate and as an astronaut, with his sense of service to Florida shining through with every word of his speech. He yielded the mic to Andrew Gillum, who is certainly no slouch when it comes to inspiring oratory.

Former Vice President Biden, though, really stole the show in my opinion. "Uncle Joe" is an apt moniker, and he spoke to the audience like they were family. He didn't speak to us like elementary schoolers, a tactic that was all-too common for national Republican leaders, and he didn't shy away from lofty concepts of service. It was evident that he had decades of experience as a public speaker, and he used every ounce of that experience to make sure the rally ended on a high and patriotic note.

Once the speeches and reminders to vote were completed, the three men descended from the stage to "work the rope line" and speak to people in the first few rows of the crowd. You've seen this on TV and in movies, when politicians walk near the event barriers, shaking hands and having brief conversations. I watched them come down the stairs, excited that I might get a chance to shake a quick hand, and as soon as he hit the floor, Joe Biden headed straight for me.

"I like your hat, did you serve?" the former vice president said, reaching to shake my hand.

"I did, sir. And I very much enjoyed your speech," I was surprised I was able to even reply.

"Thanks. You know, my son served, too. Where were you stationed?"

"I did three years on a submarine, and a combat tour in Iraq," I told him.

"Well, son, I appreciate your service," he said, looking me in the eyes and clapping me on the shoulder before moving down the rope line. Suddenly, I was acutely aware that I was still a sweaty mess from canvassing that morning. Unshowered, unshaven, and unkempt was never how I pictured meeting the former Vice President of the United States. I hoped he didn't notice.

I've said it before, and I'll say it again – the political structure in the United States is a lot flatter than anyone could possibly believe. I was just a simple state house candidate in a race that I was projected to lose, but here I was having a quick chat with one of the most powerful people in the country, all because I snuck into an event I was never invited to in the first place. I was certainly happy that I picked up the phone when Jason called me earlier that day – what an opportunity! I started the day with a plan to knock on 40 doors and make calls for the afternoon, but it ended it with a memory of a lifetime.

It just goes to show that the life of a candidate changes rapidly (as do the conditions of any political race). Be flexible. Be ready. Answer that phone call. Go to that event. Make the most of your time. You never know when the political gods will favor you with a blessing.

Adam's fundraising total: $61,573

Joe's fundraising total: $196,774

CHAPTER TWENTY

The Final Stretch

Andy Johnson, Christie, Adam, and Bryan Farris
Photo used with courtesy of the Hattersley Family

Chapter 20:

The Final Stretch

Two weeks left until Election Day, and we were in the final stretch. In my county, early voting sites open 14 days before the General Election, and more people were marking their ballots each hour. Now, on top of phone calls, knocking on doors, various events, and with every other campaign-related activity, I added waving "Adam Hattersley" signs at the various early voting sites in my district to my list of daily chores. If I ever had extra time, I could be found waving a sign at passing cars, either alone, or in a group with other candidates and volunteers.

Campaign contributions were also (finally) accelerating. The results of the poll our DEC had run must have been making their rounds in Tallahassee because in those final weeks, I received some unexpected checks from groups headquartered in the state's capitol. I had no illusions that they believed in me; they were just hedging their bets in the unlikely event that I won. Did that bother me? Nope. Was I still going to put their money to good use? Better believe it. In fact, 28% of *all* my campaign resources arrived during the last two weeks before Election Day.

Beyond late-in-season campaign checks, certain outside groups had also decided to "play" in my race in other ways. Christie and I were pleasantly surprised when a political mailer showed up in our mailbox, extolling my virtues over that of my opponent's. We started seeing independent online ads urging people to vote for me, as well. Chris and Bryan told me that outside organizations frequently took part in political advertising, but none of us thought that any of those groups would risk their money in my traditionally red district. Not just because it might be wasted, but Bryan didn't think that any of those groups would want to catch Republican ire by supporting me, especially if I lost. Maybe there were some people out there that believed in us just as much as we did.

"Did you know people were going to send mail out for you?" Christie asked me after we received our second "Adam positive" third-party mailer.

"Nope. Which is a good thing – by law, candidates aren't allowed to coordinate with third-party groups for stuff like this. These organizations can send all the mail they want, provided it's independent of our campaign. Those are the types of rules that send you to jail if you break them, so we've been careful to stay compliant," I told her, still shocked that anyone would care enough to spend money on a race like mine. "I'm done with calls for the day, too, so I'm going to head to the closest early voting site for some sign waving."

A short time later, I was at our local library, which also happened to be the largest early voting site in my district. Hundreds of people cycled through each day casting their ballots, and two judicial candidates set up a tent each morning for candidates to congregate, wave signs, and greet voters. Both Democrats and Republicans hung out with the non-partisan aspiring judges, all trying to make a positive final impression on voters, many of whom were still undecided about (and unaware of) the down-ballot races and their candidates.

So late in the election season, most candidates were friends by now, too, regardless of their party affiliation. True, I wanted my fellow Democrats to win their elections, but that didn't preclude me from being cordial with "the opposition." After all, wasn't that what the Founders of our Nation intended? But in a culture that increasingly tells us that different political philosophies must lead to conflict, it was refreshing that none of the races in my area, mine included, had gotten too negative.

Sign waving with the judicial candidates was also, strangely enough, fun. There was a small concrete island in the library's parking lot where they set up every day that became the unofficial candidate hub. It was far enough away from the actual polling location to comply with state election laws while providing a good vantage point to greet every single car that came to the library. With the addition of a beach tent, cooler, and a radio, it was the perfect spot for sign waving. We became a small family in that parking lot, helping each other and having the inspiring political discussions usually reserved for the movies. Our spirits seemed to lift just by participating in that group; it's a small detail about running for office that I'll never forget.

Conditional Help

With only 11 days remaining until Election Day, my old campaign trail buddy, Phil Hornback, and I hosted our last fundraising event together. Phil had arranged for a local jazz trio to perform, and I handled the food and other logistics. In all honesty, we weren't expecting this event to do much more than pay for itself, and it was akin to a graduation party in that we were about to graduate, from campaigning, at least.

Most of the attendees were some of our strongest supporters, lending more credence to the gathering's informal air. They had all seen us, some multiple times, over the past several months, and they had heard our stump speeches before. There was no need to persuade this group.

Out of courtesy, candidates keep the local party informed of any public activities, and this event was no different. We had let the DEC and its various committees know about our "end of season" finale and hoped some members would join us. As always in political circles, the larger these events were, the better. So, neither Phil nor I were surprised when the DEC Chairwoman showed up. Like Phil and I, she made the rounds greeting and chatting with everyone; it was networking at its finest. Toward the end of the evening though, she approached me with Bryan in tow.

"I have good news for you two," she whispered conspiratorially. "I talked to the county party's finance committee, and with the strength of your latest poll, we decided to invest an additional $4,500 in your effort."

"That's fantastic! We have a contingency plan to use extra funds if, and hopefully when, they come in. I know just where to put $4,500 to make the best use of it," Bryan said, beaming.

"Well, here's the thing," the Chairwoman said. "The finance committee really thinks the best way to use the money is for a mailer directed at NPA voters over the age of 55."

"That's *not* in our plan, and it's not the best strategy to win. $4,500 will reach about 9,000 voters by mail; if we put it into digital, it could reach 100,000 voters multiple times," I said with great conviction because of course, by this time, I knew my stuff.

"The finance committee has their own plan. If you don't want $4,500, I'm sure we can find another candidate who could use the money with the *guidance* the committee is trying to give."

Bryan already got it, and I began to understand. The county had $4,500 for my campaign but *only* if we used it how *they* wanted us to use it, and not how it could be best put to use. When it came right down to it, it was help (regardless of how helpful it would be), so I was ready to accept it. As the saying goes, nothing comes for free in politics.

"We'll take all the help we can get," Bryan told her. "I'll have Chris get a list together of NPAs over 55 years old and have him design a mailer. If you can get us the money, we could have it ready to go in two days."

"I'm so happy to hear that! I'll make sure to have a check for you tomorrow," the chairwoman said, before gliding away to the snack table.

"What the hell?" I asked, turning to Bryan.

"I hate when this happens; people not involved with a campaign who try to meddle in it. I'm honestly not sure we have enough time to even put this money to the task they're dictating. It's almost wasteful, especially when we could make it work for us so much better. I get the feeling that this late-game interest in your race is only so the county can claim credit for your victory if you win," he said with a scowl.

It turned out that the county party wasn't the only group looking for last-minute laurels in the event of a Democratic win in the 59th.

House Victory Enters the Game

Florida election law is complex. It holds campaigns to vastly different standards than our national laws do, so understanding what is required of down-ballot candidates can be tricky. One Florida campaign finance law was about to rear its head in every non-federal election across the state: a candidate cannot accept any campaign contributions within five days of their name appearing on an election-day ballot. That meant that we had a hard cutoff approaching; November 1st was the last day we were allowed to fund raise in anticipation of the November 6th election. Every candidate was scrambling hard for the last dollars of the 2018 election cycle, and I was no different.

Chris, Bryan, and I had a plan to eke out every inch of every last dollar I could raise by sinking it into digital advertising. More and more, that's the best "bang for the buck" in political advertising, getting more ads in front of more targeted voters than any other method. Was it the most effective advertising method? Probably not. But digital's greatest advantage for an underfunded campaign like mine — it's comparatively cheap. Besides being inexpensive, it's also extremely flexible; we could create an ad and have it in front of voters' eyes within an hour. It's the perfect vehicle for last-minute campaign cash to produce an effect.

Sure enough, November 1st rolled around. I spent the morning making last-minute-effort fundraising calls, but Christie and I had a lunch planned with some friends. Nothing like a nice, relaxing meal on a patio while enjoying Florida's beautiful Fall weather to lower the stress levels, right? Halfway through lunch my phone rang; it was from a Miami-based caller. I excused myself from the table to answer.

"Hello, this is Adam," I used my standard greeting for unknown callers.

"Adam? Hi, this is Kionne McGhee, the incoming Florida House Democratic Leader and the head of House Victory."

House Victory is the arm of the Florida Democratic Party dedicated to electing people to the Florida House of Representatives. They were heavily involved in several state house races, investing over $50,000 each in some of their highest priority seats. As the person slated to lead the Democratic Caucus in the upcoming legislative term, Kionne had the final say in House Victory's strategy and where they put their money. Up until now, I couldn't even get a call returned from anyone at House Victory.

"Representative McGhee! It's great to hear from you," I said tentatively, suddenly feeling a bit nervous.

"How's the race looking in the 59th? I've seen some positive numbers coming out of that district, but it's going to be tight. How confident are you?" he asked.

"I'm optimistic. The demographics are with us, and I think this is finally the year the 59th is going to flip

Democrat," I told him. No matter what their outlook is, a candidate should always answer the "Are you going to win?" question positively. *Always.*

"That's what I wanted to hear. I'm going to email you my finance guy's info, call him with your bank account information and House Victory is going to wire you $4,000. You have to do this as soon as we hang up. I'm sure you know today is the last day we can give you any financial help."

"That's great news, I can't thank you enough! I'll get my info over to your guy as soon as I get his details," I excitedly said.

"Perfect. I'm also going to send one of my staffers, Neil Spencer, down to Hillsborough County the day before the election. Use him as your own staffer; he'll be ready to help out with anything you need going into Election Day." Kionne kept the good news coming.

"Absolutely. We're going to win this down here, and I'll see you in Tallahassee," I said before hanging up.

Finally! The State Party, albeit late as hell, was getting involved in my race. Even my knowledge that only $4,000 wasn't *really* getting involved, and that they were giving that token amount simply to claim credit if I won (just like the county party would), couldn't deflate my excitement. I was getting good attention and felt like a serious candidate. Christie was just as excited as I was when I got back to our table and told her about the call. Bryan, however, was a little more skeptical.

"You know they just want to "claim" you, right? They want to *claim* that they had a hand in your win... *if* you win... and *when* you win," he told me when I called him with the good news. "It's so late in the game, we'll be lucky to use it all by Election Day."

"I'm sure you and Chris are up to the task. Now stop raining on my parade!" I said, so we both got a good chuckle out of the situation. Late in the game or not, getting that call from House Victory was a huge confidence booster going into the last five days of my campaign.

Final Plans and Good Omens

Amy Bolick, Christie, and I sat down at the local coffee shop three days before Election Day to go over our final plans. Amy had done an intricate and individual analysis of each of the 47 precincts that made up the 59th Florida House District. She knew which precincts needed last-minute attention, which precincts we could expect our best turnout, and which precincts required an Election Day presence. She was also coordinating with Chris to ensure our digital efforts were geolocated to maximize their benefit. Amy was on top of her game.

Amy was also detailing the finer points of her plan that Christie and I would be responsible for on Election Day, going down the precinct list one by one, when she suddenly stopped.

"I know this has nothing to do with, well, anything ... but can I tell you guys a quick story?" she asked.

"Of course! We're all family, here," Christie said, taking a sip of coffee.

"So, when I was analyzing the precincts, I kept getting drawn back to precinct 828 for a bunch of reasons. First off, it's our biggest Democratic-leaning precinct, so we can really run up the score there. 828 has been the best performer for our team every election I've looked at. Second, it's not just Dem leaning, but it's *huge* population-wise, so at least one of you needs to spend some quality time at their polling place on Election Day.

"Here's what gets me, though. I went on the first date with my now wife on 8/28, and then we got engaged the following year on 8/28. I know it's crazy, but the number 828 has popped up in my life positively so many times that I just have a really good feeling about that part of the district. It's corny, but there's just something about 828. It's going to be our good luck charm," she told us.

Christie and I looked at each other, and she shrugged, then turned to Amy and said, "I'm totally on board with that. If thinking like that will give us the energy to keep working and help us get across the finish line, then I'm all in."

"Good. Since that precinct is so big, I'll add an extra E-Day stop for Adam to visit their polling place. The other precincts that Adam needs to visit at least once that day are 852, 959, and 972. They're all places where we can run up the score, so they need attention too," Amy said, jotting down notes while making final adjustments to the plan.

"Perfect. Anything else we need to know?" I asked.

"One more thing. You know that Republicans like to vote on Election Day more than voting early, so they're going to catch up a bit. Like clockwork, the last three elections all saw the Republican candidate gain 1,000 votes on the Democrat in this district from when early tallies were announced compared to the final result. That means that if we're ahead by 1,000 votes or more when the early results come out, we have a great shot at winning." Amy had really gotten down into the weeds in her analysis, which (as an engineer) I absolutely loved.

We were in good shape and felt like we had a solid plan. Now, it was time to execute it.

Election Eve

The night before an election is a special time. There is no countdown to midnight like on New Year's Eve, and no long-standing family traditions like Christmas Eve. Election Eve is a flurry of late-night activity and last-minute panic. Nerves fray, tempers shorten, and arguments run rampant. Sound fun? The best way to mitigate some of these effects, like most other balms in a campaign, is to have a good plan. Again, remember (and practice) the seven P's: Prior Proper Planning Prevents Piss Poor Performance.

Besides Election Day, Amy had planned for Election Eve as well. The last ritual for any campaign is planting yard signs at as many (hopefully all) polling places in the district. For us, that meant 4-5 signs at each of the 47 polling locations – a big undertaking requiring manpower. The polling places are spread out over a wide area, and to avoid any campaign shenanigans, the last-ditch sign efforts typically don't even begin until after 10:00 p.m. We had put out a call for volunteers and had commitments from several people, bringing our sign-planting effort up to seven groups ... assuming everyone showed up (which was a huge assumption since, up to this point, we never had all committed volunteers show up to anything).

Christie and I prepared the signs and greeted Amy and her wife when they arrived at our meeting site (our house). Amy had each polling location mapped out with the most efficient routes between, and she had made discrete plans for four, five, six or seven sign-planting groups. All our bases would be covered no matter how many people showed up to help. Close to 10:00 p.m., our volunteers started arriving. Our neighbors, Nick and Martin, already veterans of the giant sign project, were first to "Sign HQ," followed closely by Neil Spencer from House Victory. With five sign-planting parties already there, Amy saw her plan coming together, so she started giving out instructions. Right after Amy began the explanation though, two more cars turned onto our street, our last volunteers! Jaime and Justice rounded out the entire committed team – we took it as another good omen that every single volunteer showed up, since getting 100% attendance is virtually unheard of, especially when you're asking people to *start* helping late at night.

With seven teams, that left each with a lighter load of only six or seven polling stations each. Amy smiled as she took out her "best case" folder and handed out the routes it contained.

"With more teams, these assignments shouldn't take each group more than 90 minutes to complete," she said to the gathered ensemble. "We really appreciate all of you helping us, and don't forget to take and post photos of planting your signs! *Let's get this done!*"

We went to our respective vehicles after Amy's mini pep talk and focused on our purpose. Christie and I went out together and made our way to the first of our six assigned locations. We were covering the Northeast section of the district and darted off to one of the largest public schools in the area to decorate our first polling place.

Upon arrival, we once again realized the absolute insanity of what we had gotten ourselves into when we were greeted by a forest of colorful placards. With well over 200 signs from every campaign imaginable already planted, we were going to be hard pressed to find any available real estate for our signs. Most of the other campaigns started a little earlier than we had apparently.

"What the hell?" Christie said under her breath, looking at the unintentionally abstract display lit up by the headlights of our car. I was equally stunned by the confusing cacophony of colors before us.

"So many signs basically negate the value of any sign, don't they? It's a sign forest! No one is going to pay any attention since it's so noisy," I said.

"I think you're right! But the thing is, any missing name becomes more conspicuous for simply not being there. I guess we still have to play this stupid game. Let's find spots for your signs and get this over with," Christie replied. She was right.

This scene repeated itself five more times at five more polling places. Just as it did for countless candidates and volunteers at thousands of polling places across the country that night. Fortunately, Amy was right in her estimates, and we finished posting the last sign just before midnight. Each volunteer let us know when they were done, too. Photos had been posted, social media had been updated, and official voting locations had been...

littered? All that was left was to head home, go to bed, and try to get some sleep.

Not surprisingly, sleep didn't come easy that night. The next day's outcome was the culmination of *months* of effort by so many people that believed in me. Thoughts of both hope and doubt fought each other in my head, keeping me awake. Had we done everything in our power to win? Even though it was far too late to be questioning our strategy or actions, my self-inquisition just wouldn't be held at bay. Did we raise enough money? Had we put that money to the best use? How were our ads being received? I was over analyzing and I knew it, but at this point, what harm could that do?

Election Eve is stressful for any candidate. It's normal. Thoughts of doubt are natural when facing the judgement of thousands of people. Me or him? This or that? Yea or nay? A candidate's fate rests solely on that simple choice. Nerves are expected to be raw. Embrace the uncertainty, that's the only path available, so you might as well go down that road with your head held high.

Adam's final fundraising total: $78,512

Joe's final fundraising total: $223,759

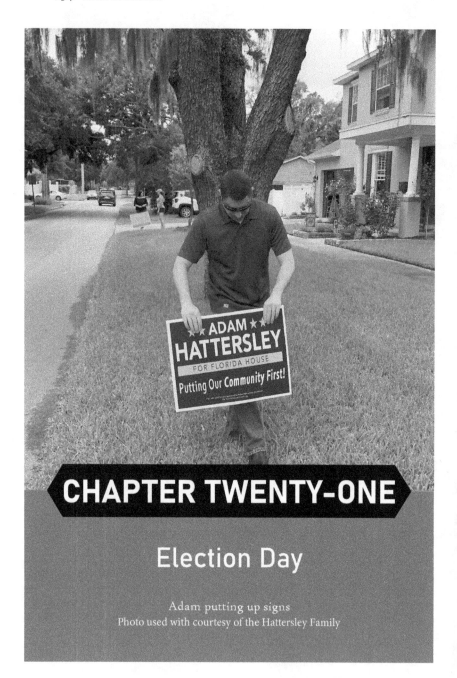

CHAPTER TWENTY-ONE

Election Day

Adam putting up signs
Photo used with courtesy of the Hattersley Family

Chapter 21:

Election Day

Here it was! We had *finally* made it to Election Day. I felt like a kid on Christmas morning, except it would be an excruciating 14 hours of work and stress before I could open a present. And at the end, that present very well may be heartbreak. Sound fun?

Polls were scheduled to be open from 7 a.m. to 7 p.m., and according to Amy's plan, I would be visiting 13 different polling places, and two of those twice each. Photos and social media posts would follow my (and Christie's) progress all day, showing happy voter interactions and testimonials. No one knew if it was it too late to further influence any voters, but we weren't going to let any opportunity pass us by. We were not going to stop punching until the final bell.

Before leaving home on our respective treks, Christie and I made little additions to the signs we planned on waving. I added a cut out "I Am" to my "Adam Hattersley" sign, and Christie added a "My Husband Is" placard. We hoped showing personal involvement might make an impact. Voters were used to seeing volunteers waving signs, but with our additions, we were making it visibly known that the candidate and his wife were out and about. No better way to show you care about the community than by being out in the community.

With the final touches to our signs in place, we headed out to follow Amy's plan. Actually, we first stopped at the local coffee shop for a latte (to get that energy up) *before* getting to our first polling stations – it was before 7 a.m., after all, and sometimes, it's the little things that help get you through the day (and I would need all the help I could get this particular day). By the time I parked at my own precinct's polling place, Amy had already let me know that she was in place at her assigned spot, and we had volunteers headed to more locations. Shortly after, Christie checked in to let us know she was at her first station and that lines were already forming by the time she got there.

Time ticked away, and polling places all over the state had opened their doors. Ladies and gentlemen, start your engines – let's get today's race underway!

Between waving my sign and greeting voters, I chatted with three other campaign workers that were there representing their own candidates. One of whom looked familiar; the Republican staffer who shifted the balance in my favor at the Riverview Chamber of Commerce event.

"Good morning! Happy Election Day," he said, almost too chipper for how early it was.

"Hello! Good to see you, and thanks again for your help at the Riverview forum," I said.

"Happy to help. This is my polling place, and in fact, I was one of the first in line this morning. I just voted for you about five minutes ago. You're the only Democrat I voted for; I thought you did a great job with your campaign."

A quick "thank you" was all I could think to say. You always hope to get people from the other side to cross traditional party lines to mark their ballot in your favor. Those rare and crucial cross-party votes can have a major impact on any election since they count not just for you as a +1, but it's also a vote your opponent is relying on but not getting, so a -1 for them. In that sense, they can be thought of as counting double. I hoped that the day would be full of pleasant little surprises just like that one. Five hours and seven stops later (including my first stop at the local VFW Post to pay a college student for his four hours of sign waving on my behalf), it was time for lunch. Amy, Christie, and I had planned to meet at a local pub for some solid American food to go along with the spirit of the day. We stayed in touch so were able to coordinate our respective arrivals – after all, less waiting leads to more efficiency. Thus far, no one outside my campaign team had tried contacting me, which was not unusual for me, but it seemed a bit strange for a candidate on Election Day. The three of us found a table and started recounting our morning's adventures.

✱✱✱

Comments from Christie:

My heart goes out to everyone who has been a spouse on Election Day. Next to the candidate themselves, being a spouse or partner is probably the hardest job on that day. For however long your partner has been running, you feel like you have been in a perpetual state of motion. Every day is either a crisis or a triumph, and there aren't many days that are in between, so you're put in the position of absorbing those feelings both good and bad. You become the ballast in their life, the one solid thing they can rely on in a storm of uncertainty. You're their rock and the one constant that will be there, win or lose, after this whole thing is over.

I think that's why marriage in politics is so hard. It is an inherently unbalanced relationship. Adam and I, however, are unconditionally supportive of one other and our careers, goals, and hobbies. We also went into this as a team because together we could do so much more than one person. In this case, our one goal was the same: To change the world in our little corner of Florida, and to do that, we needed to get Adam elected.

It all came down to this day. You can't change the results on Election Day. You've either done the work or you haven't.

I woke up on November 6, 2018 cautiously hopeful. We planned that each of us would stand with signs outside different polling places and give out palm cards to those who wanted them. I would have preferred to have spent Election Day with Adam, but we needed all the bodies we had to cover as many polling places as we could.

I was assigned to a church in Brandon which was one of the largest polling places in the area. On my way, I turned on Spotify and blasted the "Gillum for Governor" playlist in hopes that he might pull out a win in this election. It felt like it could happen, and the music made me feel like anything was possible. I had felt the enthusiasm of everyone I met during the campaign, and after personally meeting him, I was hopeful that Democrats could finally turn this purple state firmly blue.

I got to the church, parked, and walked up to the cone to ensure I was in line with the way people were walking towards the entrance, but far enough away to comply with the law. There were two other people in the parking lot. One was holding a sign for a County Commissioner's race, and we just nodded to each other. The other was a pretty blonde woman who was sitting in a chair holding a Trump sign. I introduced myself and let her know that while we were on opposing sides, I always liked meeting new people and respected anyone willing to stand (or sit) at a polling location because we should all fight for our beliefs. We talked a little about her kids and schools, but tried to stay away from competitive politics. We then just stood on opposing sides waving at people and answering questions if asked.

About mid-morning, a woman, taller than me with a blue polo shirt, shorts and a Disney hat on showed up. She walked right past me with her table and balloons and set it up on the grass. I was a little worried because she hadn't really spoken to anyone and seemed to be on her own. I didn't want to disturb her but was really curious which way her political leanings lay.

Then, she put out a "Gillum/Nelson" sign and some Democratic palm cards. Realizing it was safe territory, I walked over and introduced myself. I said, "Hi, I'm Christie Hattersley," and pointed to the sign, "My husband, Adam, is running for State House."

She had a look of surprise and said, "OH MY GOD! YOU'RE CHRISTIE?! I CAN'T BELIEVE WE HAVEN'T MET! I'M WITH INDIVISIBLE!" (Indivisible is a progressive liberal group). She then gave me a big hug and said, "I'm Marcy. Put your signs out and your stuff down!" I was overwhelmed by her positivity and, quite honestly, it was so nice to just have someone to talk to that was like-minded. We had mutual friends in common and she told me that the night before, she and her Indivisible group had put out additional signs for Adam as they were supporting him for the seat. Our conversation warmed my heart and made the rest of the morning so much more pleasant. We *discussed people we knew, the election, and worked together to help people who were looking for information on Democratic candidates as they came to our table. If they didn't walk up, we just waved and asked them to vote for Hattersley, Gillum, and Nelson.*

✳✳✳

Spending time waving political signs at a polling place on Election Day is always a grab bag. Chances are, half of the people you interact with will love you, and the other half may want to hit you in the face. Yes, really, or at least it seems that way. At least my team (and especially my wife) had been physically safe – if we could get to the end of the day with that still true, then no matter the election outcome, it would be a successful day at the polls as far as I was concerned.

When Christie finished the tale of her morning, my phone rang with the always exciting "Unknown Caller" on the screen. I was surprised that someone other than my team would call today (so chances were strong that it was a telemarketer), but I answered anyway.

"Hello, this is Adam," I used my typical greeting.

"Hi Adam, this is Nikki Fried. I wanted to call to see how your day is looking, and to wish you luck," said the woman on the other end of the line. Nikki was running for a cabinet position as the Commissioner of Agriculture and Consumer Services and was the Democrat's best hope for winning a statewide election. We had met once or twice on the campaign trail when she made stops in the Tampa Bay area.

"Thanks so much for checking in! The day is going about as well as you'd expect; we're spending a lot of time talking to voters. Based on the turnout numbers, I'm feeling cautiously optimistic. How are you doing?" I asked.

"About the same! I think the statewide races are going to be closer than close, so we're on pins and needles. Best of luck today!" she said before clicking off. I relayed the conversation to Amy and Christie.

"Wow, very sweet of her!" Amy said. "Has any other candidate or elected official called today?"

"Nope, Nikki was the first," I answered.

"Hopefully not the last by the end of the night," Christie added.

Unexpected Worries

The three of us headed back to our house, better known during the campaign as "Hattersley HQ," after lunch to rest up. The time between 1:30 p.m. to 3 p.m. is typically the slowest at the polls on Election Day, so we planned to power nap while we had the chance. Like I learned in the military: rest when you can because you don't know when you'll get the next opportunity.

The moment we walked in the door, Christie and I both knew something was wrong. Our Australian Shepherd, Patton, never fails to greet us when we come home. Where was he?

"Patton?" Christie called out. "Where is he?" she asked, turning to me. Our pup loves Christie more than life itself, and almost nothing keeps him from answering her call.

"Let's check his normal napping spots," I said. We found him laying down at the top of the stairs, shaking like a leaf.

"My poor baby! What's wrong?" Christie asked him, bringing him in close for a hug. "What's wrong with him?" she said, looking up at me as though somehow, I was also a veterinarian.

I knelt down beside them both, gave Patton a pet, and felt his little body quaking. "I don't know, maybe he ate something bad?"

"Let's take him outside, but if he doesn't stop shaking, I'm taking him to the vet," Christie said. We took him outside. He did not stop shaking. Christie grabbed her car keys. "He's never acted like before this in his entire life, I'm really worried. I'm taking him to the doctor. You stay here; I'll call if I need anything."

I went back inside; Amy was already asleep sprawled out on our couch. There wasn't much I could do but wait, but now with even more nerves than the day already called for. I searched all over the house to see if Patton had gotten into anything he shouldn't have, and didn't find one suspicious thing. Did he get into something when we were on a walk? Did he get bitten by a spider or stung by a wasp? The poor guy only weighs 50 pounds, so a venomous critter could be dangerous.

***

Comments from Christie:

Still decked out in my Adam Hattersley t-shirt, I packed Patton into the car and went to the vet. They took us as a walk-in appointment, and Patton was still shaking. They took him to the back to do some initial tests and then brought him back into the exam room. A few minutes later, the veterinarian walked in. She has known Patton since he was a puppy and has seen him through a few crises before, like when he got into the closet and ate half a bag of his food or the time he cracked a tooth while playing frisbee.

She walked in and sat down on the floor with him. Surprisingly, he let her pet him while she gave him some treats. She looked up at me in my chair and said, "I think Patton is okay, but I think he may have had an anxiety attack. Dogs can feel stress in a home. Is everything okay?"

I looked at her while wearing my "Adam Hattersley for State House" t-shirt and said, "Stress? It's Election Day!" She laughed and said, "That's right! Well, then I would suggest you both just go home and get some rest. Patton will be fine, and he seems settled now. Call us if there are any other issues."

So, with instructions of rest and relaxation on perhaps the most stressful day of our lives, Patton and I loaded ourselves back in the car to go home.

✳✳✳

Christie came in the door with a happy-looking Patton in tow, but a scowl on her face.

"The vet said there's not one thing wrong with him physically. You won't believe this, but she said he was having an anxiety attack – the vet even asked if there was anything stressful going on in our home today since animals tend to mirror our emotions. I cannot believe it!" she reported.

"Damn, I guess pets really can empathize with us," I smiled and tried to lighten the mood. We had experienced a lot of stressful days during the campaign, but our dog had to pick today of all days to show his empathy? Poor little guy wasn't going to like it when we left him home by himself again in about an hour.

Christie and I trundled off to try and finally take that power nap, and of course, Patton was right on our heels. Our rest time had been cut in half, but at least Patton was okay. It's the little things.

Back to the Polls

Short nap and minor pet emergency complete, it was time to head back into the hot Florida sun to visit more polling places. We had three and a half hours of the busiest voting time of Election Day to make our pleas to marshal the campaign across the finish line.

The first place I went was back to the local VFW post to pay the second college kid for his time waving an "Adam Hattersley" sign that afternoon, and while I was there, I did a little sign waving myself. The VFW Post was in one of the district's smaller precincts, but that didn't mean it wasn't worthy of our attention.

The rest of the afternoon was spent much like the morning, travelling from one polling place to the next based on Amy's plan, speaking to voters and posting more on social media than I ever had before. I ended my day at the same location where I started, my own precinct's polling place. It is a massive church that serves one of the most populated voting areas in the district, and no matter the outcome of the overall election, I, at least, wanted to win the precinct where I lived.

The sun was setting on Election Day, and the polls were only scheduled to be open for another 30 minutes, but in that short time, nearly half of my neighbors showed up to vote. Each one greeted me with a smile or a thumbs up and told me they were headed in to mark their ballots for me. Even though several of them were Republicans, they *still* had my back, and that's something else I'll never forget.

By the time our neighbors had come and gone, the time to cast ballots on Election Day 2018 was over. I let out a huge sigh of relief; no matter what happened when the final tallies were announced, win or lose, as of that moment, the campaign was over.

I went home exhausted but knew that the day was far from over. Christie had gotten home a few minutes before me and was nearly ready to go to our election watch party, so I jumped into the shower to rinse off the grime and sweat of the day. When I emerged, my phone was ringing. It was our strategy and digital guy, Chris Mitchell.

"Adam, it's Chris. Where the hell are you?" he quickly asked.

"It's only 7:20, I just got out of the shower. Why?"

"I'm at your watch party; hurry up and get over here! Early returns have you up by 2,800 votes!" he said excitedly before hanging up.

Holy shit! I might win this thing after all.

Adam's early vote total: 23,510

Joe's early vote total: 20,685

CHAPTER TWENTY-TWO

The Results

Adam and Christie when they learned he had won the election
Photo by Lise Emilcar

Chapter 22:

The Results

I sat down on the bed, not really believing what Chris had just told me. I thought back to Amy's analysis that determined we had a shot if the early returns had us at least 1,000 votes up.

"What did he say?" Christie asked me.

"We're ahead," I barely choked out. The realization that seven months of hard work might unexpectedly pay off hit me a lot harder than I thought it would.

"By how much?" Christie knew Amy's numbers as well as I did.

"2,800 after mail-in and early balloting."

"Holy shit! We have to get to the party!" Christie screamed. "Get dressed!"

I quickly dried off and threw some clothes on, gave Patton a reassuring pat, and ran out the door behind Christie. We were hosting a joint watch party with three other candidates: two running for the state house besides me and a candidate for the county commission. We banded together since none of us were favored to win, so we figured that we would consolidate our defeat in one place

- the same place we had all watched Andrew Learned lose his primary election, which was only half a mile from my house. The early returns gave us hope that the location's losing streak would be coming to an end.

We walked into the venue with our nerves tingling but were warmly welcomed by a loud cheer from the 80 people already there. They had been watching the theater-quality projection of the news on the wall (again, same setup as Andrew's party) and knew that I was in the lead. Christie and I waved to the crowd and were immediately surrounded by Chris, Bryan and Amy. To no one's surprise, she had her laptop open to the Supervisor of Elections' webpage and was tracking the precinct by precinct returns.

"It's looking good!" Bryan said as he hugged me.

"Nearly half of the precincts have already reported, and you're still in the lead," Amy said as she tried shoving the laptop in front of me to emphasize her excitement.

"We should know definitively within the next hour, for sure," Chris chimed in.

"Is this really happening?" I asked. "Where are Phil Hornback, Debbie Katt and Andrew Davis? How are they doing?" Those were the other three candidates sharing the party with us.

"The news has already called Andrew's race; he lost pretty bad but that was expected. He's sitting in the back of the room by himself. Poor guy," reported Bryan, letting us know as quietly as he could. "I think Phil's and Debbie's races will be called soon, too, with the same result. Everyone has their hopes pinned on your race now, and the Senate and Governor's races of course."

"How are those races looking?" Christie asked.

"It's far too early to guess. Both races are neck-and-neck," Chris told her.

Suddenly, the crowd erupted in a cheer, and my eyes snapped to the news broadcast in time to see my race being updated in the ticker at the bottom of the screen. I was still ahead with 64% of the precincts reporting, although my lead had shrunk to 2,200 votes. We were still in good shape.

I found Phil and Debbie, two of my closest campaign trail buddies. They were both in good spirits even though their races were all but over. Phil's campaign manager, Jason Marlow, however, was not taking the loss very well. I sat down next to him right when the news made the call in Phil's race. His face fell from disappointment to obvious despair when the graphic making Phil's loss official appeared on the screen.

"You guys ran a good race and did all you could," I told him. "The district was just too Republican, but you should be proud of what you accomplished."

"I know. And honestly, I never expected to win but for the last two weeks, I let that spark of hope burn a little too much. Toward the end, I thought we had a chance. It's looking promising in your race though, and I'm really happy for you but I need to go home. I don't want to cry in front of everyone." He looked on the verge of tears already. He had a quick chat with Phil, then bolted for the door. Poor guy, he had really laid his heart on the line over the last several months.

Results Are In

Bryan made his way over to me and leaned down to whisper in my ear, "Wait two minutes, then follow me outside. Christie, Amy, and Chris are already there, and there are only a few precincts left to report." He didn't want anyone getting overexcited if they noticed my core campaign team huddling up. After all, we weren't totally out of the woods yet.

I chatted with a couple more people before heading out. Amy was on a bench just outside the party frantically refreshing the Supervisor of Elections' website, with the rest of the group around her. When she looked up and saw me, she had a tremendous smile on her face.

"Remember how I told you the number 828 is special to me, and I had a feeling about precinct 828? Well, all but one precinct in the district has reported, and the only one left is 828 – which is one of the biggest Democratic precincts in the entire district! There's no denying it now... **YOU WON!**" Amy said in an excited rush.

"Oh. My. GOD!" Christie yelled and hugged me. Bryan, Chris, and Amy all joined in on one of the most meaningful group hugs of my life.

We did it.

Right as we were about to go back inside and make the announcement, my phone rang. It was my opponent, Joe Wicker. He must have been looking at the same information that we were.

"Hello, this is Adam," I answered.

"Hello Representative-Elect Hattersley, it's Joe Wicker. I wanted to call and congratulate you on your victory tonight. You ran a hell of a race." It's customary for the loser to call to congratulate and concede the race to the winner. Sometimes in bitter races, the call doesn't happen, but Joe and I both ran positive campaigns and were still cordial.

"I appreciate it, Joe. We had to run a smarter race on our side because you were in it. Let's stay in touch."

"You're my representative now, too, so don't think I'm going to lose your number!" He said before hanging up. I relayed the conversation to the group still outside with me.

"Should we go back in and make a victory speech?" Bryan asked.

"Hold on, I want to call my parents first," I said, and walked a few steps away. I was getting a bit choked up thinking about this call and needed a little privacy. I'm not going to describe this call; it's personal, but I will say that I was on the phone with my mother when she saw the TV news call the race in my favor. Her reaction and happy tears are something I'll never forget.

After finishing the call with my parents, my phone rang once again before I could even take one step back to the party. The next Democratic Leader of the Florida House and head of the House Victory fund, Kionne McGhee, was calling for only the second time since I filed for office.

"Congrats, Representative-Elect Hattersley, I just saw the results in your race. I'm glad House Victory was able to help get you over the finish line. Great job, and I'll see you in Tallahassee in two weeks for swearing in," he said. "I have a few more of these calls to make; it looks like we Democrats had a good night, yours isn't the only seat we flipped from Republican to Democrat. We'll talk soon." And just like that, he was gone. I quickly relayed the one-sided conversation to my team, who were all staring at me waiting to hear what the Democratic Leader said.

"The results aren't even official yet, and House Victory is already trying to take credit," Chris said, shaking his head. "Seems about right in politics."

"Ignore them, you have some good news to break to the crowd inside, and a victory speech to deliver!" said Bryan excitedly. Christie grabbed my arm and led me back into the party.

When I walked in the door, I was greeted with a giant graphic on the news projected on the wall with my face above Joe Wicker's, with a green check mark next to my name. The local station was calling the race in my favor – now it was official! I stared at the screen with a dropped jaw (I don't think the realization that I had won had truly hit me yet), and the room went crazy! Clapping and cheers of celebration erupted at the same time a champagne bottle popped open. With all precincts reporting, our margin of victory was 1,942 votes (incidentally, Amy's prediction of losing 1,000 votes of margin on Election Day was spot on).

I just stood there in front of the crowd, head down and trying not to cry. Christie gave me a long hug (I needed time to compose myself, so the longer the better), and someone pressed a champagne glass into my hand. I raised the glass, and the room quieted down.

"We did it!" I yelled, eliciting another cheer from the group. "We put our hearts into this race, and I can't thank you enough for everything you've done. My wife, Christie, who was the *real* driving force behind this whole effort ... let's give her a round of applause!" Christie blushed and gave me another hug. I went on to thank by name nearly everyone in the room, just like you see in movies, making sure to describe Bryan's, Chris's, and Amy's invaluable contributions.

After the race was officially called, something happened that hadn't yet up to that point of my political journey — my phone started ringing off the hook. Suddenly, everyone who had told me to "go away" or had said, "I can't waste my time on a losing campaign" wanted to renew their relationship with me. The Safety Council execs that would not even put their name behind an endorsement (usually a slam dunk for a Democrat), let alone their money, were among the first to call me. Reporters wanted a quote from me. Other elected officials that didn't have the time to meet with me for seven months (all of a sudden) wanted to meet for coffee. One newspaper journalist even called to apologize for not covering the race in his publication since he "thought it wasn't going to be much of a contest." I had never been so popular in my life.

Although the party's attendees were happy that I had won, it was awkward being the only one of four candidates at the party to have come out on top. There were pockets of sadness around the three people who did not have the outcome they had also worked so hard for. More happens on the campaign trail than most people realize. The friends you make start working together and advocating for each other. Any success that one of us has can only be attributed to the overall team effort. TV and movies make politicians out to be "lone wolves" who cannot rely on anyone but their own staff, but that's not true. In today's world, politics must be a team sport. And even though there were some highlights of the team effort, as a whole that night, we Democrats lost.

No place was the team loss more evident than in the statewide races. Attorney General was called for the Republican. Chief Financial Officer was called for the Republican. Governor, Commissioner of Agriculture, and the all-important U.S. Senate seat were all too close to call with the Republican in the lead. (All but the Commissioner of Agriculture would go Republican in recounts.) When it came down to it, we got our asses kicked, which explained why everyone left the party by 9 p.m.

Regardless of the state-wide drubbing we Democrats received that evening, it was still a great night for Team Hattersley. We understood why no one wanted to stick around and watch the Governor's mansion slip out of our fingers (once again), but we weren't ready to head home quite yet. The DEC was hosting a county-wide election watch party at a bar in the Ybor City part of town, and I had already received several calls asking if I would make an appearance. I mentioned the calls to Bryan, and all he said was, "I'll call the Uber."

A New Reality

The party in Ybor City had a similar feel to the event we had just left, somber over the statewide losses with a few bright spots for consolation. Besides my district, one other state house seat flipped from Republican to Democrat, two county commissioner seats flipped, and the state senate seat in our county was so close to flipping it was headed to a hand recount. When it came down to it, our county had performed beyond expectations.

A lot of celebratory drinks and hugs came our way that night, and I couldn't help but feel good despite the glum mood from the statewide debacle. Chris couldn't stop smiling, which was very out of character for the normally stoic digital guru, and Bryan's elation was simply indescribable (the duo was responsible for one of the county commission victories, as well). If anyone came up to talk to me, no matter how long I'd known them, Bryan would reintroduce me as "Representative Hattersley." *That* was going to take a while to get used to.

"Each Representative gets two staffers; the Legislative Aide who goes with you to Tallahassee and the District Secretary to man the local office, which you need to get, by the way. Do you have anyone in mind?" Chris asked.

I looked at Christie, who simply nodded (we had already discussed this hypothetical) and went to the bar to get some fresh drinks. When I got back to the table, I put Amy's favorite beer in front of her.

"So, have you ever wanted to work in the Capitol? Do you want to come up to Tallahassee with me and make some laws?" I asked her.

"Perfect choice," Chris laughingly said before Amy could answer.

"The Capitol? I was hoping you were going to ask," she said with a smile. "I've already been checking out places in Tallahassee to rent for the legislative session. She was usually one step ahead of me anyway, so her response didn't come as a surprise to me at all.

I turned to the other side of the table and put a second beer down in front of Cassidy Whitaker. She had worked on a winning County Commission race but had coordinated with our campaign dozens of times over the last few months and was an unofficial member of our team. It was now time to make it official.

"What do you say, want to run the home office?" I asked.

"Absolutely! I want to work in state politics *far* more than county!" she said.

"Wow! Just like that you have a great staff," Bryan said. "I bet you three will make up the best team in Tallahassee!"

"Now that that's all sorted out, it's been a long day, and it's time for us to go home," Christie announced, taking out her phone to call an Uber.

She was right, it had been a long day. Hell, it had been a long campaign, and we were exhausted from the constant commotion of the past months more than anything else. Now that I wasn't simply "that guy running for an office he can never win" anymore, but instead was Representative Hattersley, the *real* effort was now in front of me.

We made it home safely, and our dog, Patton, greeted us like it was any other night, completely forgetting about his anxiety attack earlier that day. Nothing was different for him, after all. We headed up to our bedroom the night of the most personally meaningful election of our lives, still not quite believing that I had won. I may have started the whole thing as an accidental candidate, but after that night, I was officially an accidental politician.

Adam's final vote total: 33,825 (51.5%) - **Winner**

Joe's final vote total: 31,883 (48.5%)

EPILOGUE

The End Is Just The Beginning

Adam on Swearing In Day at the Capitol
Photo used with courtesy of the Hattersley Family

Epilogue

We woke up the morning after Election Day still riding the high of our victory. I fielded more phone calls and saw my social media gain more interest than any other day of my life. To the Florida political world, I was suddenly *somebody*, but to me, the only thing that had changed was my job title.

Christie, however, was excited to see Tampa's reaction to the election results. The Governor and Senate races were headed to recounts, so no new news there, but she did find an interesting headline.

"Joe Wicker Loses to Adam Hattersley"

Wait a minute! I *won* the damn race, and the newspaper can't even put my name first? I wonder if they had a headline set with a Wicker victory, and simply changed "beats" to "loses to." I wasn't going to let it affect my day because after a long campaign, it was my first real day off in months. Besides, I had a long "honey do" list to tackle. First chore? Washing the pile of dishes next to our kitchen sink. Before I even got the water going, my phone rang.

"Hello, I'm looking for Adam Hattersley," the person on the other end of the line said.

"This is he."

"Great! Do you have Representative-Elect Fentrice Driskell's phone number? I work for the local TV news channel, and I'm trying to arrange interviews with all the new elected officials, and I understand you are on her staff. Can you help me schedule a time to speak with her?" he explained.

Wait *another* minute! At least the newspaper acknowledged that I won, but the TV station thought I was just a staffer?

"I'm not on her staff, this is Representative-Elect Adam Hattersley. I do have her contact info if you would like, though."

"Oh my gosh! I'm so sorry. I guess you should be on my list, too. I'll add you in at the bottom, and yes, please give me Fentrice's email."

Christie laughed for 20 minutes about this (and still brings it up to this day when she wants a chuckle at my expense).

Fortunately, that "relegated to the back bench" feeling didn't last very long because my phone rang again less than five minutes later. This call, though, was very much welcomed.

"Hello, this is Adam," I said, still using my normal greeting.

"Hey, Adam, Pete Buttigieg here. I just saw that you won your race and wanted to call and offer my congratulations."

"Thank you! I can't tell you how much I appreciate you coming to Tampa to help us out. I think that event really put the campaign on the map," I told him.

"I'm glad to have been able to help," he said, "There are a lot of great people in Florida, and I'm sure I'll be down in that part of the country again, soon."

"Let me know whenever you come down, it would be great to see you again. By the way, is there any truth to the rumors I'm hearing about a presidential run in your future?" I asked, trying to get some inside information.

"Nothing certain yet, we're still looking at our options," said the mayor, "I'll just say that I haven't ruled it out."

"I'm ready to help however I can. I think you'd be great, and God knows the country needs you."

"I appreciate that, and I'll keep you in the loop. Congratulations again on your win. I know you'll do a great job," he said before hanging up.

Talk about a class act! I was feeling great after that call as I dove back into the pile of dirty dishes.

Helping the Neighbors

Later that same day, Christie got a call from one of our neighbors. They had bought a new couch and needed someone to help them bring it into their house and up the stairs. Was Adam available for manual labor? Christie volunteered me right away.

"You're not as important as you think you are," she told me. After the morning's newspaper and TV interactions, I certainly wasn't feeling very important, so that fit right in with the post-election theme. Sure, let's go move some furniture.

An hour of struggle, three minor stab wounds from furniture nails, and a nearly sprained ankle later, we had completed the moving job. Out of breath, my neighbor and I shared a quick high-five.

"So, what do you have planned now that you won the election?" he asked.

"I have to go to Tallahassee in two weeks to be sworn in. Believe it or not, it will be my first time at the Capitol Building! I have no idea what to expect," I told him. "Tomorrow, though, I'm headed to the Olympic Training Center in Colorado Springs for four days to help with the USA Gymnastics Junior Program. That's been on the schedule since before the campaign."

"Sounds fun. Do they know about your new job?"

"I got a lot of support from my gym friends, so several do. I'm going to need to cut down on my judging, though. Legislative Session is the same time as gymnastics season," I said.

"Well, I for one am glad you're making the sacrifice. I know you'll do a good job for the district in the Legislature."

If neither the paper nor the TV news cared about the new Representative for District 59, I was glad at least our neighbors did.

Off to the Capitol

Per the Florida Constitution, exactly two weeks after the election the new Legislature gathered at the Capitol to be sworn in. Christie and my sister, Michelle, had planned a trip to Napa months before, so I drove to Tallahassee alone two days early (both Christie and Michelle altered their plans and were set to fly into Tallahassee in time for the swearing in ceremony, but until then, I was on my own). There were smaller events being held for freshmen legislators, as well as events within our own Democratic Caucus.

My first official meeting in Tallahassee was with the other first-term Democratic Representatives, and our new caucus leader, Representative Kionne McGhee. Thinking "politically," I donned a suit and tie (dress to impress, right?), and got to the event 10 minutes early. Once again, my Navy training bit me in the ass, as I was waiting alone for a quarter of an hour. Strike one? Then, even worse, people started arriving in casual weekend clothes. Not only was I the idiot there by myself, but I was beyond overdressed. Strike two?

As more of my new colleagues arrived, it became evident that none of them had the slightest clue who I was or that I had won an election. They had all been supported by the State Party, had all met before and had all been in touch for months. Now it seemed I may be an outsider even within my own caucus. Strike three?

It turns out that my strike-calling was unfounded (Thank God). Each and every one of my fellow newbies was warm and welcoming. We had lawyers, teachers, social advocates, and small business owners. We were a diverse group, and ready to fight. *This* is what I had in mind when getting involved in politics. Being part of a team to push our state into the future. Too bad we were in the minority.

The next morning, I walked into the State Capitol Building for the first time. Paperwork, exploring and meeting all of my fellow freshmen from both sides of the aisle took up the majority of my time. Bryan and Chris were arriving that day to be there for the swearing in ceremony as well, and a celebratory dinner. I love it when a good plan comes together.

Tired but feeling good, Bryan, Chris, and I met Christie and my sister (their flight arrived just in time for dinner) at a fancy Tallahassee restaurant called Savor for one of the best meals of my life, and perhaps one of my last days of relative anonymity in the Capitol.

Or so we thought.

It turns out, the Capitol produces a small booklet with the names, pictures, and short bios of all the legislators, and people had already been studying it. Three times during dinner lobbyists that I had never met before came up to our table to introduce themselves and offer congratulations. Now *this* was a new experience! Would I be willing to set up a meeting to talk about x.y.z.? Would I have time to come to a reception for "fill-in-the-blank" organization? Could I possibly come speak to the assembled members of "such-and-such"? Sure? Great, my office will schedule it with your assistant.

What the hell was happening?

Chris explained the purpose of the lobby corp., and how I wouldn't have a moment to myself when I was in Tallahassee. Lobbyists are paid to advocate for issues, bills and most importantly, get state dollars for their projects. There are a lot of them in any state capitol, so

I needed to get to know them. I had a lot to learn about how this place worked.

The next several months flew by in a blur. I was sworn in, assigned to legislative committees, filed bills, and got into some (good) public fights over issues important to Floridians. I still got nervous when speaking on the floor of the House of Representatives, but I saw that as a good sign that I was taking this job as seriously as it deserves. I wrote op-eds, did TV and radio interviews, and fought the good fight.

In the last week of my first legislative session, I got an interesting phone call.

"Adam, this is Congresswoman Cheri Bustos, head of the DCCC. We want you to come to Washington, D.C. for some meetings. Have you ever thought about running for U.S. Congress?"

Acknowledgments

The amount of time, thought, and effort that goes into writing a book is incalculable, and there are far too many people that had a hand in the making of this one, so I apologize if any are left out.

This wouldn't have been a reality without my editors and publishers, Lil Barcaski and Linda Hinkle. Thank you for pushing me to keep going and making every chapter better. I know keeping me on schedule isn't the easiest task in the world.

Without people like Vanessa Lester, Rebecca Myers, Darlene Ritter Goodfellow, Dave Cutler and Peter Horstman (our canvassing champions), Election Day would have not turned out as well for us as it did.

The other candidates on the trail with us, win or lose, were amazing inspirations to keep fighting. Public servants like Fentrice Driskell, Ben Diamond, Rick Kriseman, Sean Shaw, Dianne Hart, Susan Valdez, Kimberly Overman, Pat Kemp, Mariella Smith, Andrew Warren, Cindy Stuart, Alex Sink, Betty Castor, Sam Bell, Amanda Murphy, Janet Cruz, Lisa Montelione, Luis Viera, Guido Maniscalco, Jack Gutman, Robin Fuson, Bob Doyel, and candidates like Debra Bellanti, Debbie Katt, Phil Hornback, Andrew

Davis, Scott Hottenstein, Andrew Learned, Kristen Carlson, and Kathy Lewis – I'll be forever grateful for every one of you. There are far too many to list, but each of you made this journey just a little bit better than it would have been without you.

Campaign staffers (regardless if you were on my campaign or not) who mostly volunteered their time to make the victory in this campaign possible. Jason Marlow, in particular for taking on the burden of all of East Hillsborough County, beyond just the district you were being paid to oversee.

Two people stayed on the journey with me from candidate to elected representative: Cassidy Whitaker and Amy Bolick. I would not have been half as successful without you, and I could not be prouder of how you have both grown in the political world.

Chris Mitchell lent his digital and political expertise to the effort, helping both Christie and I navigate a world we never knew existed. Thank you for guiding us and making our advertising dollars go as far as they possibly could.

As for Bryan Farris, thank you for taking a risk on a political unknown. I couldn't have asked for a more adept and loyal person to help us find our way to the State House. I'm sure we'll have more trips together on the political merry-go-round.

My extended family supported us from day one, and I'm grateful for every single one of you. My parents, Roger and Rosalyn; my sister, Michelle, and her family; Christie's parents Frank and Wendy; and her brothers Matt and William (and their families). Together, you kept our eyes focused on what was important and were part of the inspiration that started us down the political path.

Lastly, I cannot thank anyone more than my wife, Christie. She has done more for me as a man, as a partner, and as a politician than any other 10 people combined. Honey, I love you. Thanks for encouraging me to "do something" when it came to running for office so I could make a difference.

Appendix

Me Too No More Speech

Good morning and thank you all for coming out today.

There are moments in American history which transcend our national conversations and political discourse and offer us the ability to reveal truth.

Some of those truths, however, have been hard to face and even more difficult to act upon. We experienced it in the early 1900s with women's suffrage, we experienced it in the 1960s with the civil rights movement, and we experienced it yet again when our nation accepted same-sex marriage as the law of the land. In those moments, we looked inward and recognized our faults and our mistakes and we stepped up and said, "This is wrong. This is unjust. This is un-American," and we made a choice to do better and to seek stronger justice for Americans who were suffering or marginalized.

I am convinced that today we are experiencing one of those moments. For the last few years, we have been ensconced in a conversation about misogyny, consent, and rape culture. We have hashtagged our beliefs, from #Me Too to #Why I Didn't Report, with myriad other rallying cries in between. We have attempted to have a credible and meaningful conversation about the silent scourge of sex crimes that have poisoned the lives of millions of women, and not an insignificant number of men. But every time we feel we've gained some new ground, some new insight, we are faced with proceedings like that in Washington, D.C. that endorse and condone behavior that is cruel and criminal.

Well, Washington can do what Washington wants, but in Florida, that ends today.

Today, in the second half of the second decade of the 21st century, we live in a country in which nearly 1 out of every 5 women will be sexually assaulted at some point in their lives—and barely 6 out of every 1,000 suspected rapists will ever see the inside of a prison cell. Some research has shown that upwards of 9 out of every 10 sexual assaults go unreported, and in 8 out of 10 cases, the victims of sexual assault know their assailants. Suffice it to say, our leaders have been doing an inexcusably atrocious job of putting actual criminals—people charged with sex crimes—in prison.

These are daunting, terrifying numbers. That being said, pursuing solutions to these problems aggressively, thoughtfully, and relentlessly is the only means we have to stem the tide of sexual violence that has scarred our generation and threatens to scar the next.

We are also aware of the toxic nature of these crimes, and the copious amounts of time it sometimes takes survivors to speak up about those crimes. Survivors and law enforcement, scientists and researchers, as well as the vast majority of survivor advocates all agree that the effects of sexual assault last not for days, but for lifetimes.

It is time for us to stand up and say NO MORE. Not. On. Our. Watch.

So today, I am announcing, alongside some of my valued colleagues in the Democratic Party, the concept for a broad legislative initiative to send the message—with ONE voice—that Floridians will no longer be silent.

Instead, we will lead, and master this moment, with decisive action. If elected, I will work with my colleagues cooperatively to craft the plan in more detail, but today we will start with the basics.

Our legislative package — called Me Too No More — has three parts designed to eliminate obstacles to prosecution, provide law enforcement the best tools for our fight, and fast-track much-needed evidence in ongoing prosecutions.

The first part is simple and obvious, and it is a step that has been taken by 20 other states—Me Too No More will eliminate any future statutes of limitations for all sex crimes in the state of Florida. For far too long, Florida's sexual assault survivors have lived with the crushing reality that the criminal justice system was closed to them. By eliminating these ridiculous restrictions for the next generation, we will open a door for survivors that will lead to closing the door on serial rapists who continue to offend.

The second part is critical to give law enforcement better tools and training with which to arrest and prosecute sex criminals. Over the past few years, law enforcement agencies have begun adopting the game-changing investigative protocol known as FETI — the Forensic Experiential Trauma Interview. This technique, developed for the U.S. Army by one of its sex crime investigators, is a dramatic paradigm shift that teaches investigators the science of trauma, and its effects on the brain and victim responses. It eliminates the traditional and unconscionable interrogation of the victim and replaces it with a victim-centric approach that enables them to piece together the facts of their attack without shame or humiliation. It also helps investigators piece together better narratives that can be used as compelling and convincing testimony in court. And for the naysayers who seem convinced that every rape report could be a false accusation, this scientifically proven technique is far more effective in revealing false accusations than browbeating someone who has just suffered a life-altering trauma.

The third part of ME TOO NO MORE will find innovative ways to use public/private partnerships to fund the testing of the thousands of rape kits that have clogged our justice system and hindered prosecutions. While the Florida Department of Law Enforcement's efforts to take care of the more than 8,600-kit backlog have been admirable — leaving only 2,000 backlogged kits to be tested — as of last January, 4,000 NEW kits had been entered into the system. FDLE reports it is testing 99.9 percent of new kits within the four months allowed by law and many much quicker, but we can still do better. (Take a beat). We need laws and funding that outpace the actions of sex criminals, so we can stop playing catch-up and start simply catching them and putting them behind bars.

When my team and I first began discussing this issue, I wrongly assumed that there must be a reason why others have failed to enact these basic, simple and obvious measures before. When I looked at existing statutes of limitations on the books in Florida, and I saw so many different classifications for sex crimes and different statutes of limitations for them, it hit me. In Florida, our law books actually rank sex crimes to determine how long someone can report them, as if there is any kind of sex crime that is better than another sex crime. The absurdity of rating sex crimes on a sliding scale made me sick to my stomach. And I began to realize that there is absolutely no element of this issue that isn't fundamentally heinous. Then, I dug into the statistics. Of course, the nearly 1 out of 5 women being raped shook me, and then I looked further and saw that 4 in 10 Florida women have been victimized by sexual violence other than rape.

I didn't know that, because we don't talk about these numbers. We don't talk about this issue. And the women who know the most about it, the survivors, can't talk about it, for the most part. And then I understood ... it's the silence and the ignorance that protects rapists and haunts their victims, so I choose to act.

I am sure that skeptics will claim that we can't afford to take these measures. But make no mistake — as much as sex crimes are a plague on our state, changing the lives of their victims forever, it is also an economic and business issue.

The American Journal of Preventive Medicine published a study just last year in which it revealed the estimated lifetime cost of rape was $122,461 per victim, or a population's economic burden of nearly $3.1 trillion over victims' lifetimes, based on data indicating that 25 million U.S. adults have been raped. Government sources pay an estimated $1 trillion of that lifetime economic burden.

One footnote — the average cost of a single FETI training session for a law enforcement agency is about $5,000.

My point is this — to many who have been following the Kavanaugh confirmation process, this nonsense isn't new. Regardless of how you feel about it, the fate of women's rights is hanging in the balance. The issues are serious, the stakes are high, but our resolve is greater because it has been seasoned by decades of toxic misogyny.

I am sure I will be asked why isn't a woman standing here proposing these ideas and speaking out. The answer is simple — they have, for decades. This is not my bandwagon. I am simply joining the millions of women and thousands of female lawmakers, activists, advocates, and public leaders who have been courageously fighting — often at their own peril — for stronger laws and enforcement efforts.

But I am not here to rally women, because they don't need me to do that. They have been rallying around this issue since before I was born. I am here to rally men to join them as I am doing. It is our responsibility to be their allies and their advocates. As a man, I cannot speak FOR women, because I cannot possibly understand their journeys. I do not have a frame of reference for the fear, humiliation, pain and suffering that they have been made to feel by the pervasive rape culture that acts as a petri dish to cultivate sexual predators and provides them a welcome environment in which to thrive.

I, like the vast majority of men, have never been a victim of sexual violence, so I am unable to feel this fight as deeply as women do. But while I cannot speak FOR women, I can speak UP, and do what I can to add my voice to theirs and ensure that their pleas for change are heard and transformed into action.

I welcome my Democratic colleagues here with me today, and I issue a challenge to Florida Republicans to suppress their partisan reflexes and join us in an effort to bring Florida into the 21st Century when it comes to how it deals with sex crimes and sex criminals.

Together, we can and we will make ME TOO NO MORE the LAW, and in doing so, set the stage for a more effective and hopefully decisive battle against evil.

Thank you.

Adam & Christie Hattersley

About the Author

Adam Hattersley earned B.S.E. and M.S.E. Degrees in Aerospace Engineering from the University of Michigan and spent eight years as a nuclear submarine officer in the United States Navy. In honor of his father who volunteered for a tour in Vietnam while in the Army, Adam volunteered during the height of the Iraq War and was deployed on the ground with a U.S. Army unit, receiving the Bronze Star for his service.

Adam completed his Navy service as an electrical engineering instructor at the U.S. Naval Academy in Annapolis, MD. He then moved to Riverview, Florida in 2009 where he worked for a Fortune 500 company for seven years relying on his data-driven background to lead a team responsible for training and managing hundreds of skilled technicians all over the world. In 2016, Adam and his wife, Christie, opened a promotions business helping other small businesses market themselves.

In 2018, after more than a decade as a registered independent voter, Adam sought and won a seat in the Florida Legislature as a Democrat. Focusing on issues that matter to people across our community, Adam served in the Florida House of Representatives where he fought to lower health care costs, protect victims of sexual assault, honor the service that veterans have made to our country and protect public education.

Adam Hattersley is a member of the Selective Service Board and is an internationally certified judge for Men's Gymnastics. He has represented the United States at competitions and events on four continents.

Adam is available for speaking engagements.
Contact Adam and learn more about him on
his website – AccidentalPolitician.com